Advance Pra
Becoming the Kind ˻˻˻˻˻˻

Amid so many voices calling on men to be tough, to be manly, Calvin Sandborn calls on them to be kind, to be human. I pray that it is his voice that will prevail.
— Rabbi Harold Kushner,
author of *When Bad Things Happen to Good People*

Becoming the Kind Father is an inspiring autobiographical guidebook to the development of heart in men... *Kind Father* delivers a hopeful message of healing, both for individual men and our angry culture. It has been said that in our culture "real men" cry bullets instead of tears, but this book suggests a more hopeful vision. It suggests that real men cry tears when they are sad, they sing when they are happy, and ultimately and most importantly real men are kind.
— Frederic Luskin,
from the Foreword

Professor Sandborn's well-referenced book is crammed with valuable self-help tips that when practiced will help debunk society's macho myth and give birth to the real man who is loving, sensitive, gentle, and kind.
— John Bradshaw,
author of *Homecoming, Creating Love,* and
Healing the Shame that Binds You

In this remarkable book, story and lessons-learned are finely woven together. Narrative passages of memory and observation are moving, and beautifully written, while the author's suggestions for individual growth are both reasonable and wise, with the strength of extensive research and personal experience behind them.
— Jack Hodgins,
author of *Broken Ground* and *A Passion for Narrative*

A must-read for anyone who has imagined practical alternatives to the destructive energy of their own or a father's chronic fury. As one who has walked the walk before talking the talk, Calvin Sandborn understands that angry men are made not born and that nurturing compassion for oneself is the key to choosing to live free of anger's burden. *Becoming the Kind Father* has the hallmarks of a classic-to-be: true-life stories, vividly related, that deftly illustrate important truths men can use to enrich their own everyday lives and, consequently, the lives of those they love.
— David Greer,
   author of *Simple Pleasures* and *A Book of Wishes*

As fathers, we spend a tremendous amount of time and energy trying to make our children happy and trying to be heroes to them. In the process, they never get to know who we really are. In *Becoming the Kind Father*, Calvin Sandborn takes the reader on a journey of self-discovery that, ultimately, will help us be better men and better fathers.
— Armin Brott ("Mr. Dad"),
   author of *The Expectant Father* and *Father for Life*

Becoming
the **Kind Father**

Becoming
the **Kind Father**

A Son's Journey

Calvin Sandborn

NEW SOCIETY PUBLISHERS

CATALOGING IN PUBLICATION DATA:
A catalog record for this publication is available
from the National Library of Canada.

Cover design by Diane McIntosh. Image: iStock.

Printed in Canada.
First printing February 2007.

New Society Publishers acknowledges the support of the
Government of Canada through the Book Publishing Industry
Development Program (BPIDP) for our publishing activities.

Paperback ISBN: 978-0-86571-582-0

Inquiries regarding requests to reprint all or part of
Becoming the Kind Father should be addressed to
New Society Publishers at the address below.

To order directly from the publishers, please call toll-free
(North America) 1-800-567-6772, or order online
at www.newsociety.com
Any other inquiries can be directed by mail to:
New Society Publishers
P.O. Box 189, Gabriola Island, BC V0R 1X0, Canada
1-800-567-6772

New Society Publishers' mission is to publish books that contribute in fundamental ways to building an ecologically sustainable and just society, and to do
so with the least possible impact on the environment, in a manner that models
this vision. We are committed to doing this not just through education, but
through action. We are acting on our commitment to the world's remaining
ancient forests by phasing out our paper supply from ancient forests world-
wide. This book is one step toward ending global deforestation and climate
change. It is printed on acid-free paper that is 100% old growth forest-free
(100% post-consumer recycled), processed chlorine free and printed with
vegetable-based, low-VOC inks. For further information, or to browse our full
list of books and purchase securely, visit our website at: www.newsociety.com

NEW SOCIETY PUBLISHERS   www.newsociety.com

Contents

To Baby Brighton
and his generation
of men in the making,

And to the beloved
Nicole, Kathleen and Kristen.

Acknowledgments

I would like to acknowledge my mother Lucille who gave me unstinting love; and brother Tom, who came closest to being a Kind Father. Without them, I would never have had the confidence to embark on this journey.

I am grateful to Jack Hodgins, one of Canada's finest writers, for his kind mentoring and sage advice as I developed this book. I also deeply appreciate the generous and perceptive editorial assistance that authors Bob Armstrong, David Greer and George Sranko provided. Betsy Nuse has been a deft and adept editor. I want to recognize the contribution of the late Stanley Boggs, the high school English teacher who taught me to love writing and Shakespeare.

I am deeply indebted to Terrence Real for his groundbreaking research into the dysfunction of modern men. His book, *I Don't Want to Talk About It*, first opened my eyes to many of the issues that I discuss.

I want to express my deep appreciation to Graham Archdekin, Steve Feldman, Don Frenette, Tony Kost, Bert Lamsa, Phil Mesner, Chris Parks, Scott Petersen, Cory Porter, Sarah Verstegen and Nikki Wright, for their comradeship and emotional support.

Special acknowledgment goes to mentors Neil Solomon, Peter McLean and Candy Porter. They have guided me through hard times and enriched my life beyond measure.

I am grateful to my childhood friends who knew some of the background of this book, and provided helpful memories and comments. My thanks go to Jupe Barceloux, David Duncan, Joel Hawthorne, Evan Lichlyter, Robert McKee, George Mowles and Stephen White — and to my sisters Pam Sandborn and Fran Snodderly.

I want to thank the many friends who expressed confidence in this project from the start, and offered useful feedback on early manuscripts. Their comments encouraged me to continue, and provided invaluable assistance in shaping the final book. These friends include Merv Aramenko, Claus Brandes, Al Brown, Daryl Brown, Susan and Peter Chandler, Rick and Donna Cook, Kim Eden, Kevin Edquist, Kathy Foster, Dick and Rosalia Ginsburg, Kelly Green, Russ Haas, Mark Haddock, Linda Hannah, Randy Hein, Maria Helena Hernandez, Hannah Horn, David Johns, Deb McLeod, Paul Millar, Simon Owen, Neela Paige, John Pennington, Norah Reksen, Michael Robinson-Dorn, Robin Ruffell, Leslie Waters and Mike Wyeth. I am particularly indebted to Gail Rogers for her insight, assistance and support.

I also wish to acknowledge the helpful comments from my colleagues at the University of Victoria including Ben Berger, John Borrows, Oliver Brandes, Hamar Foster, Don Galloway, Rebecca Johnson, Maxine Matilpi, Michael M'Gonigle, Anne Pappas, Murray Rankin, Chris Tollefson, and Liz Wheaton.

Finally, thanks to Chris Plant of New Society Publishing for his faith in this book, and to all the New Society staff who have contributed to its publication, including Judith Plant, Sue Custance, Ingrid Witvoet and Ginny Miller.

Foreword

Becoming the Kind Father is a memoir of a tragic father-son relationship and its ultimate reconciliation. It is also a work of literary imagination, marked by reinvented vignettes from *Moby Dick, The Wizard of Oz*, Shakespeare, Greek myth and Hollywood movies. Realistically its value is as a practical book that provides men with useful self-help tips to kindness, reconciliation and forgiveness.

The book does this through a recasting of the male *Hero's Journey*. Since ancient times this legend has shaped men's lives and dominated their culture, but *Becoming the Kind Father* takes the Hero down a wholly different path. The quest that Sandborn invites men to join is not a journey to conquer distant lands, save damsels, or fight dragons, but a quest to reclaim the male heart and come into relationship with their loved ones and the world. As men struggle in a post-feminist culture for updated myths, many will welcome this helpful guidebook to a new quest.

Kind Father is an inspiring autobiographical guide to the development of heart in men, and a worthy companion for men who choose to pursue this journey. An appealing feature of the book is that Sandborn is a lawyer, not a psychologist, and thus he is not just describing abstract recommended practices. He writes from personal experience, describing what it feels like *inside* to apply the useful psychological approaches. The other advantage of the book is that Sandborn is a gifted writer who holds the reader's attention.

Becoming the Kind Father first deconstructs the harsh training fathers inflict on sons, and documents the sad price men pay as a result. The book cites evidence of the damage done to men as they play out the male role of hiding their feelings and their grief. The toll of male suicide, alcoholism, disease, shorter lives and emotional alienation make a good case for wanting to change; and it is my hope this book will induce men to consider altering their lives and the lives of their sons.

The book is first and foremost personal, and is structured around recollected scenes from Sandborn's own painful relationship with his father. When the author's 25 year marriage collapses, he finds himself confronting his own anger, and discovers the extent to which he has adopted his father's anger as his own. As Sandborn explores his own self-talk, he is surprised to discover he has incorporated his father's hated voice, and the hardened voice of Everyman, into his inner dialogue. As with many men, Sandborn projects this harsh inner dialogue into anger at his family and friends. The project the author sets out is to change that destructive conversation with himself.

The turning point for Sandborn comes when the author confronts the ghost of his dead father, and asks the Old Man to leave, thus ridding himself of the critical "tapes" that he hears of his father's voice. Then, with a spark of creativity pioneered by Berkowitz and Newman, the author sets out to be a Kind Father to himself. Quite simply, he decides to start speaking to himself in the encouraging, nurturing way that a healthy parent speaks to a child.

The author carefully chooses the best qualities from all the men he has known and synthesizes them into an ideal internal mentor, a "Kind Father." This parent is one that only a fortunate few know in real life. In subsequent chapters the author recounts how he learns to parent himself and leads the reader through his experience of personal growth. Each chapter is an essay on a theme, a meditation on a step in the journey to a man's heart. The steps include the ways a man learns to identify his feelings, ways to share his feelings with friends and loved ones, techniques to free himself from excessive anger, and finally tools for learning and practicing forgiveness.

With forgiveness as his guide the author achieves something genuinely useful, a friendly relationship with himself, characterized as a transformation from alienated anger to self-acceptance. Again with forgiveness as his guide a final reconciliation with his long-dead father ensues, and the book makes clear the author has grown stronger, and finally is able to see that his life is beautiful and full of joy.

Sandborn learns that difficulties need not lead him only to anger, isolation, and contempt, but can be lessons in opening the heart and connecting with others.

> *Like most men, I was ashamed of speaking my pain. But I've discovered life's sweet, redeeming secret — a secret that many women know, but that patriarchal society hides from men. The secret is this:*
>
> *Sharing my sorrow with others creates an unsuspected bridge from my heart to theirs. Simply by listening to each other, we can transform sorrow into something joyful — empathic connection. This connection is one of the greatest gifts that life offers.*

Becoming the Kind Father heralds a new masculinity, one that is not defined by the sword, but by gentleness and kindness. It is a masculinity that recognizes that patriarchy often destroys men emotionally and physically. *Becoming the Kind Father* recognizes that male power does not only come from the repressive anger and control that men have so often exercised. Male power can also emerge when a man knows himself, has learned how to take care of himself and opens his heart to goodness and forgiveness. This power comes when a man learns to be open to himself and his feelings, rather than neglecting his feelings while trying to control others.

Kind Father delivers a hopeful message of healing, both for individual men and our angry culture. It has been said that in our culture "real men" cry bullets instead of tears, but this book suggests a more hopeful vision. It suggests that real men cry tears when they are sad, they sing when they are happy, and ultimately and most importantly real men are kind.

Like many women who read the *Feminine Mystique* forty years ago, some of the men who read this book are going to recognize themselves and will want to change themselves and their relationships. *Becoming the Kind Father: A Son's Journey* is an alternative to outdated models of masculinity that our stressed and angry culture sorely needs.

— Frederic Luskin, Ph.D.
    Author, *Forgive for Good*
    Director, Stanford University Forgiveness Projects

Prologue

The Hero's Armor

When Theseus turned 16, his mother took him aside. "Son," she said, "Today I will tell you who your father is."

They left the familiar palace garden and walked in silence, deep into the dark woods. When they finally broke into the sunshine of a small meadow, she took his hand. "I promised your father I would introduce you on the day that you became a man."

"They tell me my father is Poseidon?"

She looked at him curiously, then shook her head. "No son, your father is not a God. But he is a Hero."

They walked on until they came to a small emerald lake. On the shore was a massive granite stone, and the mother motioned the youth to sit next to it. She drank from the lake, rinsed her face and then stood looking pensive. Finally she stepped between him and the sun.

"Theseus," she said softly, sunlight framing a harsh halo around her hair, "your father is King Aegeus of Athens. And he wants you to inherit his throne."

Immediately, the youth jumped up, "Damn him! I've never even seen this King!" He picked up a rock and hurled it into the lake, muttering, "Why did he leave me?"

"Before you were born, he was called back to war." She smiled wanly. "But the day he left, he brought you and me to this very place." She paused, walked over and squeezed the youth's hand. Then she pointed to the large boulder.

"He took off his royal armor and put it right here, under this boulder." She looked Theseus in the eye. "Then he stroked my belly where you lay, and told me this: 'When my son is man enough to retrieve his armor, he may come to me and claim his throne.'"

Theseus stared at his mother, then at the stone. "I will go meet him," he said. Without another word, he strode over and pressed his shoulder against the rock. It didn't move. He redoubled his effort, until the veins on his neck and arms stood out. He breathed deeply, dug his feet into the soft grass, and gasped. The stone moved an inch, then a foot. It teetered for a moment. Finally, with a mighty shove, Theseus pushed it over.

There before him, in a hollow in the ground, lay sandals, a finely carved sword and a suit of bronze armor. Theseus knelt down and quickly put on the sandals, then the armor. As the armor glinted in the sunlight, he picked up the sword and held it high.

"Well done," his mother said. "Now, go to Athens and present yourself to your father." Immediately Theseus set out to cross the dark and dangerous wasteland that lay between him and his father.

My Father's Heart

From the time I was a small boy, I knew that someday I must wear my father's armor. Like all my friends, I knew that someday I would enter a dark forest, lift an impossibly heavy stone, and put on the armor that passes from father to son.

Like most fathers, Dad never let me know him. He was preoccupied by life in Athens. However, he managed to bury the armor, and leave me instructions.

His sword helped me make my way in a dark and dangerous land. But the ancient armor formed a small prison around my heart.

Patriarchy's Price

Then they bring them to the factory
Where the Heart Attack machine
Is strapped across their shoulders . . .

And the only sound that's left
After the ambulances go
Is Cinderella sweeping up
On Desolation Row.

— "Desolation Row," Bob Dylan

Have compassion for modern man.

With only one life to live, he cannot feel it. A chunk of his heart has been cut away. As he confronts life's natural shocks, he cannot feel his heart's response. He can conjure anger, but is blind to his own sorrow and fear. He seldom feels joy.

He is the Great Pretender. Embarrassed by his feelings, he presents a mask to the world — a stoic mask of what a man *should be*. Showing the mask to friend and foe — and even to himself — he takes the secret of his tender self to the grave.

He is a stranger to his own inner life. When he looks inside himself, no one's home. He is insensitive, sometimes cruel, to himself. He treats himself like a machine, a body with a job to do.

Intimacy is beyond his ken. Though surrounded by people, he is lonely.

Yet he strives to love in the only way he knows. Keenly aware of duty and obligation, he strives to be a good provider and protector. He spends his life "in harness." He drives himself, he performs, he achieves.

He believes that he must be a Hero. He competes to be the best stud, husband and father; to have the biggest house, finest team and lowest golf score; to have the prettiest wife, finest career, smartest kids and flashiest car. He believes that the whole world is divided into winners and losers — and that if he loses he will be worthless. So he won't give himself a break.

Tragically, his life is not his own — it's a performance for outsiders. He simply cannot see his life through his own eyes. Instead, he constantly tracks his reflection in the eyes of spectators.

Like Narcissus, he is so obsessed by his reflection that he can't see the woman who loves him. And like that Greek, mesmerized by his own image, he ignores his real needs and starves to death.

Indeed, the cost of traditional masculinity is high. It destroys our health and our hearts:

The State of our Health

- The life span of the average man is approximately six years shorter than that of the average woman.[1]
- Men commit suicide at a rate four times that of women.[2]
- Two–thirds of all alcoholics are men, and 80% of those with alcohol-induced liver disease are men.[3]
- Virtually all stress-related diseases — from hypertension to heart disease — are more common in men than in women.[4]
- Men's heart disease and cardiovascular disease death rates are about twice as high as women's, prior to old age.[5]
- Almost 90% of all ulcers are in men.[6]
- Compared to women, twice as many men die from accidents,[7] and three times as many die from homicides.[8]

- Being male is the single largest risk factor for early death. Before age 50, for every 10 premature female deaths, 16 men die prematurely. If male death rates dropped to the female rate, one third of all male deaths under age 50 would not take place.[9]

What is the reason for this pattern of ill health? A big part of it is the traditional "masculine" role, and the way men are taught to deal with feelings. We're trained to react to emotional stress in a way that creates significant health risks. While women relieve stress by sharing their problems with friends, men are ashamed to share and internalize the stress. As a result, men are far more likely to have premature heart attacks. In addition, macho culture encourages men to turn uncomfortable feelings into anger — which swells the number of men felled by accidents, homicides, suicides and heart attacks. The male ritual of using alcohol and drugs to drown feelings just adds to the damage.[10]

A recent study in the *American Journal of Public Health* concludes that the modern concept of masculinity is helping to kill men:

> What are the factors for the higher rates of morbidity and mortality among men? Beliefs about masculinity and manhood...play a role.... Men are socialized to project strength, individuality, autonomy, dominance, stoicism and physical aggression, and to avoid demonstrations of emotion or vulnerability that could be construed as weakness. These cultural orientations...combine to increase health risks.[11]

Other studies have confirmed it — the masculine role is a hazard to men's health.[12]

The State of our Hearts

Even more tragic than the state of our health is the state of our emotional lives. The men who drink themselves to death or commit suicide are obviously emotionally desperate. But noted psychologist Terrence Real estimates that *almost half of all men* suffer from some form of covert or overt depression.[13] He attributes this to the way that men are socialized to deny their feelings.

Many of us trudge through life, feeling numb inside. Because of our social training, we have lost contact with an Inner Life. In fact, psychologist Ronald Levant estimates that close to 80% of men suffer from some form of alexythimia — the inability to identify what one is feeling.[14]

The mechanic who knows every nuance of the internal combustion engine, the physicist who unravels mysteries of the universe, the lawyer who recalls two centuries of common law — each may go home puzzled, unable to distinguish whether that big feeling inside is anger or sadness. Men simply don't know what we feel.

This alienation from feeling has been described by Dr. Robert Pasick as "Men's Deep Sleep". It even extends to being cut off from physical feeling — an alienation that Dr. Henrie Treadwell cites as a significant cause of male mortality:

> Becoming a man in this society means living with the pain, ignoring the pain.... Quite simply, men...are largely out of sync with their own bodies.... [15]

Unable to feel their pain, men don't get medical help when they need it. And they often die as a result.

Of course, a man who doesn't know what he's feeling can't possibly express his real feelings to others. He can't tell them what he wants, or who he really is — because he doesn't know. Thus, for many, genuine connection with others cannot take place. These men live in profound isolation, cut off from their own hearts — and the hearts of their family and friends. Men routinely fail at close relationships. For example, close to half of all marriages end in divorce — and 80% of those divorces are initiated by the woman.[16]

Out of touch with their inner lives, disconnected from others, many men fill their lives with addictive behavior. They become addicted to drugs or alcohol. They become addicted to their work. Or they become obsessed with television, the internet, sports, gambling, compulsive sex, acquiring things — anything to divert themselves from painful feelings. Other men numb their pain with chronic anger. Or they keep their feelings in check by obsessively controlling those around them. Many sink into the abyss of depression.

In sum, emotional disconnection kills many men — and it condemns millions more to grey, lonely, distorted lives. It clearly doesn't have to be this way. But to change things, men are going to have to come to terms with a concept that makes most red-blooded men cringe — *patriarchy.*

Patriarchy– Cutting Boys in Half

In our resentment against feminist criticism, men have missed a vital point. Patriarchy has stolen our hearts and is killing us.

As psychologist Terrence Real has pointed out, patriarchy forces boys into a state of profound emotional disconnection, from self and others.[17] And it is this disconnection that has such tragic consequences for men's health, their lives and their families.

Patriarchy is the age-old system where the father ruled over the family — where "the man is master of the house." It's a laddered society, with the father at the top, then the wife or eldest son, and everyone else on different rungs below.

In this system, relationships are about having "power over" others, not "being with" them. Males are on top. But even sons must defer to the father for years, before they get to the top. No one relates straight across, eye to eye, heart to heart.

To reach their destined place at the top, males must avoid being sensitive or in touch with their feelings — they must be strong and controlling, without fail. Boys must don their father's armor.

Historically, patriarchy likely developed because men and women faced different tasks. Men had to hunt, make war and protect the tribe. In contrast, women were left behind at the cave to nurture children and build a social community.

When men went out to war or to kill the sabretooth tiger, they needed to concentrate on power, control, performance and courage. Hunting parties needed leaders — and people to take the leader's orders without question. Men couldn't afford to be too sensitive. It would have been stupid to discuss your inner feelings while the sabretooth lurked nearby, or enemy mortars exploded.[18] Somebody had to be tough and in charge. Somebody had to wear armor.

As a result, patriarchal society assigned certain characteristics exclusively to men:
- strength
- power
- action
- physical aggression
- anger
- independence
- performance
- stoicism
- autonomy
- decisiveness
- production
- control
- heroism

On the other hand, women bore the children, raised them, and kept the village going as a functioning community. As a result, society assigned quite a different set of characteristics exclusively to women:
- the ability to create intimacy and emotional connection
- nurturance
- sensitivity

- emotional life
- kindness
- patience
- communication
- relationship building

Although both men and women can embody every one of the above characteristics, patriarchy demanded that people sacrifice important parts of themselves. Women were forced to sacrifice their strength and autonomy — any woman who dared show such "masculine" characteristics was promptly condemned as a "shrew," "bitch," "nag," "witch," or "castrator." Conversely, men were forced to suppress their emotional sensitivity — any man showing such a "feminine" characteristic was condemned as a "sissy," "wimp," "wuss" or "pussy."[19]

Over the centuries, a profound human tragedy occurred. Men and women were cut in half. Women lost their voices — and men lost their hearts.[20]

As Sam Keen puts it, "Each gender is assigned half of the possible range of human virtues and vices.... Every man and every woman is half of a crippled whole."[21]

Patriarchy is Obsolete — But Lives On

At one time there might have been a reason for patriarchy's harsh division of the human personality. But today we live in a far different world. Men no longer spend their lives in tribal hunting parties. Indeed, millions of women now "bring home the bacon." Most modern men don't engage in military combat. And it's the rare woman who limits her life to hearth and home.

The fact is, today's society requires *whole* human beings. Modern families require women that can coach soccer and men who can change diapers. The same is true in the workplace — modern work teams thrive when women are free to be assertive, and men free to be kind. Furthermore, we now know that individuals are far healthier if they can integrate both "masculine" and "feminine" traits.[22] And society benefits when *all* people are free to realize their full potential.

Clearly, patriarchy is an outmoded social structure. The insensitive hierarchy that served primeval hunting parties and wartime armies is no longer necessary. But our evolutionary history still resonates. "Masculine" traits such as performance and control are still primarily assigned to males, while "feminine" traits such as empathy skills are still assigned to females.

With the rise of feminism this is changing, and gender roles will inevitably change more. In recent decades many women have clearly found their voice, and many men have gotten more in touch with their emotions. However, the old paradigms remain surprisingly strong, and in the militaristic post-9/11 world are even gaining strength. As William Pollack has pointed out, even boys coming from "enlightened" neighborhoods still learn patriarchy's rulebook at an early age.[23]

And this Boy Code is what still leaves most men "half of a crippled whole."

Patriarchy's Rulebook — How the Boy Code Works Today

From the time he is about five, a boy is told to repress his feelings if he wants to be a "real boy." In *Real Boys*, William Pollack has identified the four great imperatives that society presses upon boys:

- **Never show weakness.** Men should be stoic and stable.
- **No "sissy stuff."** Don't express feelings or "feminine" dependence, warmth or empathy. Be cool. If you must show emotion, show anger.
- **Give 'em hell.** Be tough, macho, take risks.
- **Be a Big Wheel.** Achieve status, dominance and power. There are only winners and losers — don't be a loser.[24]

We find these Boy Code messages everywhere in our culture — in music, movies, literature and television. Our culture is still dominated by the ideal of the man as stoic hero. The archetype is still the myth of Prometheus — the hero who braves danger to steal fire from the gods for humankind, and then stoically endures an eagle eating his liver every day.

In fairy tales, the hero wears emotional armor as well as real armor. While he slays the dragon and saves the princess, he must always be brave. She shows emotions, but he doesn't. Instead, he is cool, powerful and "in charge." He's like Davy Crockett, "The King of the Wild Frontier...the man who knew no fear...."

It is essential that men not show feelings. The plaque on the office wall of England's last king summed up the male credo: "If I must suffer, let me be like a well-bred beast, that goes away to suffer in silence." [25]

The ideal is to become a Man of Steel, like Superman. Like steel, men are to be cool, hard, impervious. Superman is all action, all decisiveness, all performance. He is machine-like — "faster than an airplane, more powerful than a locomotive." Nothing hurts him — bullets bounce off his chest. His sensitive side is split off and assigned to the pitiful Clark Kent.

From Valentino to Bogart, from John Wayne to Clint Eastwood, from Sylvester Stallone to Arnold Schwarzenegger, male heroes are expressionless, emotionless and dominant. Many, like Batman, Green Hornet, the Lone Ranger and Zorro, actually wear masks to hide their faces and feelings.

With few exceptions, movie heroes don't show vulnerable feelings. When Clark Gable was asked to break the rules and cry in *Gone With The Wind*, he sat on the set and agonized for hours — asking repeatedly, "Would Clark Gable do this? Would Clark Gable do this?"

A classic example of the Boy Code in action is *Lethal Weapon*. This movie, like many others, teaches boys that it is actually better to kill than to feel. Suicidal over the death of his wife, policeman Mel Gibson can't express his grief.

Instead, he repeatedly toys with putting a loaded gun in his own mouth, then goes on a manic rampage killing criminals.

His only options are to kill others — or kill himself. Processing his grief is not an option. Audiences cheer as he kills, rather than feels.

Thus, our culture teaches boys that it is unmanly to be in touch with their feelings and express them. They are taught to be ashamed of feeling vulnerable, sad, anxious or lonely. Feelings are to be subordinated — they belong to the world of women or "homos." If boys acknowledge such feelings, they will be considered part of these lesser beings — and lose their place atop the patriarchy.

They are taught that to be a man they must forgo feelings and feeling-based relationship.

The Hazing

Such cultural messages do not stand alone. The Boy Code is enforced by a "hazing" process that trains boys to suppress their emotions, and to develop contempt for them. This brutal teasing and shaming begins at about age five.[26]

Fathers, coaches, teachers, peers and others conduct the Boy Code hazing. Much of the hazing consists of taunting the boy for breaking the four Code imperatives (e.g., Never show weakness; No "sissy stuff"; Give 'em hell; Be a Big Wheel). Teasing is used to enforce the message that the boy must be tough and not show emotions — he must be cool, and in control. He must be a hero.

Any man will recognize the common slogans used in the hazing process that enforces the Boy Code:

Big boys don't cry
C'mon, take it like a man
Don't be a chicken
Don't be a mama's boy
Show him you're boss
Don't be a sissy

Buck up
Baby!
Grow up
Be a real man — Fight like a man
Don't back down
Don't let them push you around
Don't be a pansy
Keep a stiff upper lip
Be cool
Be tough
Tough it out
Hang tough
Be strong
Take charge
Get over it
Stop crying or I'll give you something to cry about
Don't lose your nerve
Don't back down
Snap out of it
Stand up to him
Cut the apron strings
Don't be a dork
Don't be a wimp
Don't be a wuss
Keep a poker face
Don't cry, you homo
Don't be a girl!
Don't cry, you woman
You swing like a girl!
Don't be a scaredy cat
Get some balls, man
We're counting on you
Be your own man
Stand on your own two feet
Suck it up

Shake it off
Take it
Put up or shut up
Talk is cheap
Fight your own battles
When the going gets tough, the tough get going
Get out there and win
Winning isn't the most important thing — it's the only
   thing
Take control

When Mom left us on the first day of kindergarten and we started to cry, we were admonished — "Big boys don't cry." When we were hurt or heartbroken, we were told to "Tough it out." When our bike was stolen, when grandpa died or when our emotions were simply more than our parents could deal with, we were urged to "Buck up and take it like a man."

Often the hazing process is cruel. The classic movie *Rebel Without a Cause* illustrates the violence involved. Buzz challenges Jim to a teenage game of "chicken," where they simultaneously drive cars off a cliff. The first to jump to safety is the "chicken." Jim jumps out and lives. Buzz doesn't, and dies.

Afterwards Jim explained to his dad why he had to play the game: "It was a question of honor. They called me chicken! I had to go or I could never have been able to face any of those kids again."

Jim chose to get in his car and race it off a cliff into the sea, rather than be called a chicken by the guys. Even so, Buzz's friends later nailed the carcass of a bloody chicken to Jim's front door.

On his way to manhood, a boy undergoes some 15 years of Boy Code hazing, both subtle and brutal. And ultimately there's a high cost. By adolescence, boys have already stopped

trusting other boys. And by adulthood, a young man is un-
likely to ever again form an intimate friendship with another
man.[27]

Most destructively, the boy eventually turns the hazing messages onto himself. He learns to routinely greet his
sensitive feelings with contempt. This contempt shames him
into disowning his feelings — and the self from which they
come.

The result is akin to an emotional clitorectomy — he can
no longer feel.[28]

Putting on My Father's Armor

As the boy suppresses his real self, he replaces it with a "false
self" that fits the Code rules. This constructed self doesn't
allow itself tender feelings, or show them to others. It wears
armor.

Pollack describes this false self as the "Mask of Masculinity:"

> …a mask that most boys and men wear to hide their true
> inner feelings, and to present to the world an image of male
> toughness, stoicism, and strength, when in fact they feel
> desperately alone and afraid.[29]

As boys, we dare friends to punch us in the stomach and then
pretend it doesn't hurt. We adopt the emotionally flat voice of
a Bogart, a Schwarzenegger or Snoop Dog. We mimic the un-
feeling voice and gestures of the Marlboro Man, John Wayne,
Gibson and Eminem. Like Prometheus and our dads, we
never cry — even when the eagle devours our flesh.

Boys hide their hearts, because they've been brainwashed
to believe that their hearts are shameful. Their sense of intrinsic worth — the self esteem that says that *I have the right to
be who I really am* — has been pounded out of them.

So boys cover the shameful self, and try to prove that
they're worthwhile by Code standards. They set out to

become Big Wheels and Heroes — to impress others by winning, by asserting power and status. They try to prove themselves with performance.[30]

The man begins a constant quest to prove his worth —
with a good job, big house, fast car, possessions, portfolio,
athletic feats, trophy wife. Forgetting his inherent value as
a *human being,* he begins to see himself as little more than
a *human doing.* He is what he does. He becomes what he
achieves. Like the Tin Man in the *Wizard of Oz,* he becomes a
hollow man whose life is his work.[31]

Two tragedies result. One, when achievement falters, such
men don't have a solid sense of self to fall back on. They're
only as good as their last race. If they lose, they fall into an
abyss of shame. John Updike described it: "Women get more
out of life. Men, if you don't win every time, you're nothing."[32]

The intense pressure on men to achieve — or else feel
shame — is reflected in the health statistics.

But the second and more fundamental tragedy begins
much earlier, when the young man first accepts that he actually *is* the Mask he projects. Pretending to be what he is not,
pretending to feel what he doesn't, he finally fools himself.
And at that moment he loses his most crucial relationship
— his relationship with himself. Like most men, he becomes
unable to identify his real feelings and needs.

When he looks at himself, he sees the heroic Mask. When
he looks again, he sees a productive machine. But he misses
the tender human being inherently worthy of love. He misses
his real self.

And without that connection to self, the young man loses
the ability to live his own life. Instead, he just finds himself on
stage, reading lines from the Code script. He can no longer
connect heart-to-heart with others — because he has no idea
where his heart is.

Fathers and Sons

It all starts with Dad. Boys learn to abandon their hearts from their fathers. Men are cut off from their emotions because they never saw their fathers express their inner feelings. For generations, fathers have passed down the mask and armor to their sons.

Most fathers are either remote or angry with their sons. Shere Hite's survey of 7,239 men showed that "almost no men" were close to their fathers as they grew up.[33] In another study, Sternbach found that:

- 23% of fathers were physically absent;
- 29% were psychologically absent — busy with work, uninterested and passive;
- 18% were psychologically absent — austere, moralistic and emotionally uninvolved;
- 15% were dangerous, frightening, apparently out of control; and
- only 15% were appropriately involved, nurturing, trustworthy, warm and connected.[34]

Leading Australian family therapist Steve Biddulph confirms this, estimating that less than 10% of men are friends with their fathers and see them as a source of emotional support. Of the remainder, Biddulph estimates that 30% don't speak to their fathers; 30% have prickly or difficult/hostile relationships; and 30% go through the motions of being good sons, while discussing nothing deeper than lawnmowers.[35]

Some young modern fathers are beginning to break the mold, and choose to be supportive and nurturing with their sons. But the general rule has been that a father doesn't teach his son how to connect on an emotional level — because the father himself is shut down emotionally.[36] The father can't teach "relationship" — he never learned it from his own father, and has lived an entire life without authentic relationships.

Instead, the father teaches his son the Boy Code, the same Code the father learned as a child. He teaches his son that if he wants to be a man, he must be a Big Wheel and exercise patriarchal "power over" others — not "connected relationship" with them.

The father addresses his son from a height, treating him harshly or coldly. From this, the son learns to treat his own inner child the same. He learns to speak harshly to himself, in the same voice that his father used. The son's inner life becomes a place of harshness, coldness, sometimes cruelty. The ugliness of patriarchy is played out inside his head, as he wars against his true self.

Just as patriarchy brutalizes women, it brutalizes him. This is the cost of the father's armor.

The Hero's Journey

On the road to his father's castle, Theseus crossed the wasteland — a wilderness where notorious villains frequently attacked innocent travellers. Inspired by the fact that he wore the Great King's armor, Theseus challenged these thugs. He killed the Club-Bearer with the man's own club. He killed Procrustes on the villain's own torture bed. He hurled Sciron off the same cliff where that outlaw had killed so many innocents. He tied the Pine Bender between the two bent trees that the brute used for dismembering people — and then sprung the trees loose. When he was done, the road was safe for travellers at last.

The city of Athens welcomed the young hero, hailing him for his deeds. To honor the stranger, King Aegeus invited him to a royal banquet. But the King's evil wife knew who Theseus actually was. Fearing he would displace her son as heir, she lied to the King that Theseus was out to steal the throne — and convinced him to poison the young hero at dinner.

Just as Theseus raised the poisoned wine cup to his lips, his cloak lifted and Aegeus recognized the finely-carved sword. Suddenly realizing his mistake, the King lunged forward and knocked the cup to the floor. "My son," he hugged him, "My son is the Hero!"

Eager to serve his new King, Theseus volunteered to go kill the Minotaur that had long terrorized Athens. As Theseus departed on this mission, his father gave him a set of special white sails for the ship — and told him to hoist them in celebration after he killed the monster.

Eventually the young hero plunged into the Labyrinth and killed the man/bull. But in the drunken revelry that followed, Theseus forgot to hoist the white sails. As Aegeus kept a lookout for his son from a promontory above Athens, he saw the black sails on the returning ship — and concluded his son had died. In despair, Aegeus sobbed and railed at heaven. He clawed out his eyes, then stumbled off the cliff.

This tragedy made Theseus king, and, like his father, he went on to become a legendary warrior. But one day as he made his way along a narrow cliff face, his father's chest armor caught on a rock. The young King lost his balance, and he too fell to his death.

Decades later, the Oracle at Delphi commanded the people of Athens to find and honor the young King's body. For days they searched in vain. Finally, an eagle descended from heaven and tore at the earth, revealing all that remained — some hair, a few bones and a complete set of armor.

When these relics were returned to Athens, the people welcomed them with sacrifices and grand processions. The city celebrated the hero's armor as if Theseus himself had returned alive.

Our fathers tried to be heroes. And they wanted us to be heroes too. But the life of a hero is, in the end, a tragedy. The armored hero lives and dies alone. He is a stranger to his own son. He invites his child to drink poisoned wine. Observing the son from a great height, he misunderstands him — and as a result falls to his own destruction. Eagles pluck out his heart and flesh, leaving only bones and bronze. True, the crowd pays him homage — but they celebrate the armor, not the man.

This was our fathers' fate.

My own father was a harsh, hard-drinking, hard-swearing, tattooed man's man. He drilled the Boy Code into me, and insisted I wear the Masculine Armor. But this book is the story of how, in mid-life, I abandoned the armor and took off the mask. As I passed from hero to mortal, I began to feel again. After decades lost in man's deep sleep, trapped in patriarchy's tragic script, I reestablished a relationship with my self.

This is the story of that journey back to my heart. On the dark and dangerous journey to my home, I followed a few simple but profound steps:

- Saying goodbye to the patriarchal Harsh Father that was in my head, and turning off his criticisms.
- Becoming a Kind Father to myself, learning to encourage and nurture myself in the way that a healthy parent encourages his children.
- Learning to pay attention to what I'm feeling, and to give myself permission to experience it.
- Learning the joy and intimacy that come when I speak what I feel — and listen attentively to others.
- Learning to not escape from feelings into anger.
- Learning to forgive myself and others.

As I followed this process, I forged a comfortable new relationship with myself and the world. But that was not all. To my surprise, decades after his death, I rediscovered my father's tender heart.

A
Son's
Journey

Me, 1956

Saying Goodbye to the Harsh Father

My father was frightened of his father,
I was frightened of my father,
and I am damn well going to see to it
that my children are frightened of me.

— King George V (1865–1936)

1961

My buddies and I are playing touch football. It's a perfect Northern California fall afternoon, and I inhale the crisp air deeply, and wait for the snap.

Our pasture is a good place for a pickup game. The milk cow keeps a serene distance from the half dozen 11 year olds who kayai, shout signals and yell for the ball. The long grass softens the fall when you dive for a pass — and the occasional cow patty sharpens our feinting skills and sense of humor.

"75-40-22-45-Hike!" Jim shouts. Pretending to be R.C. Owens, I go long for the Alley Oop. Jim casts up a long, wobbly pass that falls, just beyond my fingertips. "Darn!" I spit out.

"Calvin!" I look over to the farmhouse porch, where my dad stands, hands on his hips, bellowing. "Calvin! Get the hell over here, you knothead."

"Uh-oh," Jim mutters, as the other boys begin to scatter. The kids know enough to avoid Dad. "See you later, " Jim shouts, as he ducks through the barbed wire fence.

"I said now!" Dad shouts, louder now, voice full and threatening even at a distance.

"I'm coming," I cry, placating, shoveling the football to Glenn, who trots into the trees, headed for his house.

"So is Christmas. Get the hell over here!"

I arrive at the porch panting. Dad, unshaven with a bead of spittle on his upper lip, points his finger and glares at me. "Why didn't you peel those potatoes?"

"What?"

"The potatoes for dinner… Unless you want to eat them RAW." He scratches his protruding belly. "They damn well aren't going to peel and cook themselves, Einstein." His untucked shirt rides up over his belly, as his voice rises, "Jesus Christ on a crippled crutch, can't I count on you for anything?"

"Sorry, Dad." I know better than to point out that he had told me to start the potatoes at 5 o'clock and it was only 4:30. That would just provoke him.

"You should be sorry. Your mother works all goddam day. She shouldn't have to cook the sunuvabitchin dinner too, just because you want to play, Prince Charming." He turns and storms into the hot kitchen, pulling the five-gallon pot off the shelf and slamming it onto the counter.

"Here, get to it!" He smacks the potato peeler down next to the pot. Then he storms off to the bathroom, muttering, "I swear, useless as TITS on a BOAR!"

The bathroom door slams. Moments later, I hear the toilet's water tank lid being lifted, and the clink of glass. He's fishing out the Smirnoff's vodka bottle he keeps there, hidden from my mom.

I bend over, feverishly peeling the potatoes, burning with the fear and shame that he refuses to feel, but projects so violently onto me. I'm in a panic, breathing fast and shallow. I squeeze back tears, closing my eyes so hard that I see stars.

In the bathroom my father explodes into a coughing fit, hacking violently, a vehement, gasping smoker's cough. Wheezing and choking, he desperately tries to clear his throat and get air. He hacks, and suddenly falls silent. I wonder if he's died. For a moment, dread vies with hope.

"Goddamn it," he finally mutters, clearing his throat and spitting. I hear the toilet flush.

When he comes out, he sets his horned-rim glasses on the counter, picks up a potato and peers closely at it. "Jesus Christ almighty! Look, you're missing spots here. See, see that spot there?" He holds the potato in my face. "Can you see it?"

I nod, wordless. "If it was a snake it would bite you.... They're full of spots. Now, get all the skin off those things. And hurry up, you're going to make us all late."

He pauses, looks in the cracked mirror on the wall next to the fridge, and slicks back his thinning hair with his fingers. Beads of sweat rise on his forehead. He reaches to adjust his false teeth, and the pink plate rolls in his mouth, before settling into place. He looks at himself with a trace of disgust.

Then he turns and glares at me, "Just straighten up and fly right, dammit."

1998

Thirty-seven years later, I'm at my counsellor's office in Canada, talking about an incident where I shouted at my wife. Overwhelmed by fear of losing her, I am scared. I know I was in the wrong, and I harshly criticize myself out loud:

"You're really no good... you're really fucked up now...."
I'm despairing, desperate, angry as I chastise myself. "You're not good enough. You're a fake. You just can't do it right," I continue.

"Wait a minute," Neil interrupts. "That's not you talking." I stare at him blankly.

He leans forward, and presses, "Who's saying that?"

I think for a moment, nervous, thinking I might not be able to answer. Then it comes. "My dad."

"I'd like you to close your eyes and relax... now, can you picture your dad?" At Neil's urging, I relax and close my eyes.

In the darkness I conjure my long-dead father. Like Banquo's ghost, he emerges from the shadows, a tall, heavy figure, a familiar, slack, deeply-lined face.

"Have you got him?"

"Yes."

"Good. I want you to speak to him. Tell him how it feels when he says those things."

"Dad, I don't like it when you talk like that." I pause, struck by how young my voice sounds.

Neil softly says, "Tell him what it does to you."

"I feel real bad when you say those things. It makes me feel small...." In the darkness inside my head, Dad's presence is palpable: I am quiet for a moment. "And no good, and scared." I pause and let it sink in, savoring the power of speaking.

Neil steps in to lead, echoing what I've said — "Dad, I feel bad, when you talk to me like that."

"Dad, I feel bad, when you talk to me like that." I repeat to the man in the dark. "Actually," I say, suddenly matter-of–fact and determined as an eight year old, "it *really, really* makes me feel like a jerk. I hate it."

"What's he doing?" Neil asks.

"He's listening. He's kind of bent over, and he seems kind of sad, but he's listening." I sigh. "It's surprising, but he *is* listening."

"OK, now I want to encourage you to tell him to stop."

"What?"

"I want you to stop talking to me like that," Neil coaches.

Focusing on the heavy man looming in the shadows, I repeat, firmly, "I want you to stop talking to me like that." I half expect Dad to explode into anger, but in the darkness inside me he is strangely quiet, compliant. He lowers his head.

Neil's voice, soft and reassuring: "Now, I want you to leave, Dad. You've been with me for all these years, but I don't need you anymore. Your job is done. I'm not a kid now. You don't need to take care of me anymore."

In the darkness Dad lifts his head. Haltingly I repeat Neil's words to the distant figure. I stop, then add, "You don't need to be here." When I'm done, I see something glisten on Dad's cheek. A tear?

I carry on: "I know you did the best you could. But I've grown up now, and I don't need you here. I want you to leave now. I can take care of myself...."

I raise my voice, with increased resolve. "It's time for me to go on, and live my own life. Thank you for your work, Dad, but now it's time. I've grown up. I'm going to take care of myself. I want you to go... you can go now."

Dad, somber, turns and shuffles into the distance, shoulders slumped. As he recedes into the shadowy underworld, I pity him.

But after he disappears, I feel a profound calm. Finally, Neil's voice fades in. "OK, in a couple of minutes I want you to open your eyes and come back into the room. Take your time...." I open my eyes. As I meet Neil's kind gaze and glance around his study, I feel light — like a heavy burden has lifted.

When I leave Neil's, I walk down a sunny Victoria street, smiling to myself, exhilarated. The sidewalk is lined with red and yellow tulips, and the cherry trees are fat with blossoms. A wind comes up, and a blizzard of pink petals swirls around me. The air smells sweet.

I feel like a playful, eight-year-old boy. With a spring in my step, I quickly cross the lawn in front of the ornate stone Parliament Buildings. I give an ironic nod to the statue of Queen Victoria, and another to the grimacing Doughboy, who endlessly attacks an invisible enemy with his bayonet. A horse-drawn carriage full of Japanese businessmen rolls by, and beyond it a tall sailing ship bobs in the harbor, lines clanking in the wind.

In nearby Beacon Hill Park, I stride through an oak meadow in bloom. And there in a sea of tall blue camas flowers and knee-high grass, it finally hits me. I laugh out loud, and skip a few steps down the path. Though it's ages since I last skipped, I find myself skipping and grinning into the spring day. "I should do this more often," I joke to myself, savoring the frivolity of springing off the ground.

I stop for a moment and stretch, head back and arms wide open to the sky. Above me, shreds of white cloud race across the pale blue sky. Then, lowering my head, I keep my arms extended and pretend to be an airplane. Usually self-conscious about the image I project, I find myself rushing through the brilliant camas, a kid playing airplane, making takeoff noises by vibrating my lips. For twenty yards I rush forward, dodging oak trees, dipping my wings to one side, then to the other. I dip a wing and graze my fingers along the top of a lilac bush, flushing a robin into flight. The wind feels good on my face.

I stop the airplane bit, adjust my tie, and resume walking down the path. I look around to see if anyone noticed. No one in sight. "Who cares," I say to myself. "I'm free."

My Father's Voice

The voice of parents is the voice of gods,
for to their children they are heaven's lieutenants.
                     — Shakespeare

My father lived in my head for years after he died. He was my constant companion. And he was not kind. Decades after his funeral, he continued to speak to me daily, telling me that I wasn't good enough.

Like many fathers of my generation, Dad believed that it was necessary to toughen boys up. It was his duty to correct and chastise, and he ferreted out the flaw in everything I did. He'd point at the six blades of grass I missed with the mower, as if he'd just found my victim's corpse. If I missed a spot on a single dish, I'd have to wash the whole load again, under strict orders to not talk this time. If he was having a bad day, it was impossible for me to clean the car right, or adjust the TV to his satisfaction.

Then he "gave me hell." Frustrated in his own life, he vented his sarcasm and rage at me. I was a "knucklehead" and "slackass." I hadn't tried hard enough. I was stupid and wrong. Ashamed of his lack of education, his unemployment and other failures, he projected onto me — "What's your problem, you useless tit?"

Thanks to my mother's encouragement, I achieved much as I moved through life — high school valedictorian, National Merit Scholar, lawyer, law reformer, musician, author, community leader.... But tapes of my father's voice still played in my head, and his constant message from the grave was that I was simply not good enough. If I burned the toast, I'd call myself a jerk. If I made a mistake at work, I'd give myself grief. My messages to myself mirrored his messages to me:

Oh, fuck, that was a stupid thing to do.

I'm screwing this up.

I should have known better.

Jeez - us, what's the matter with me?

I'll never get it.

I am not as smart as he is.

I always forget that stuff.

I can't handle money.

I'm not good at fixing things around the house.

I'm not good looking.

I'm getting fat — why don't I exercise more?

I'm a bad father.

I spent years calling myself names.

The amazing thing is, I didn't even know it was Dad. I just thought the self-criticism was the simple truth. When his voice spoke, I didn't recognize it. I thought it was mine, or maybe God's.

His critical voice echoed in my head, unchallenged. Scientists tell us that the average person conducts a constant interior monologue with himself, processing events as they pass before his eyes. This "self-talk" proceeds at 300–1000 words per minute.[1] Too much of my self-talk echoed Dad's voice.

At work, nothing I did was ever good enough. No matter how good the job, I'd still criticize myself for not doing it faster, or better. I took little satisfaction in my successes, focusing instead on what I hadn't done. Even if I'd clearly won a victory, the afterglow never lasted. The next hour I was off — on a forced march — to the next task.

For a career, I chose a job dead centre in the patriarchal machine. I became a lawyer. This was my life:

> During an appeal hearing I spend much of the afternoon silently shredding myself for a minor oversight, telling myself how incompetent I am. Afterward the opposing lawyer shakes my hand, assures me I will win — and tells me that my cross-examination was one of the best that she's ever seen. I am surprised. In the inner Court that Dad presided over, I got no mercy — let alone credit.

In order to counter the Inner Critic, I spent my life trying to win the approval of others. Not knowing how to give myself encouragement and comfort, I turned outside — trying to impress others and win their praise. Like Blanche DuBois, I was utterly dependent on the kindness of strangers.

If anybody criticized me, I was devastated. Any criticism whatsoever seemed to confirm His critique. So to avoid all criticism, I obsessively hid my mistakes. I became an expert at artfully wording things to leave the *impression* that I had not erred.

On the other hand, when people praised me, I couldn't really accept that either. My Internal Critic routinely discounted any positive remarks others made — reasoning that the person didn't mean it, they didn't know all the facts, they had an ulterior motive, or I had just fooled them.

My basic problem was that a harsh stranger's voice ruled inside. Every day I was hard on myself and tense with others — because my father's voice echoed in my head. The only way I knew how to talk to myself was with his demanding voice. I wounded myself and didn't know how to stop the bleeding.

Unkind Fathers — A Common Legacy

My dad was an alcoholic, often loaded and mashed. Drinking made his behavior extreme, his words bizarre. But his general approach to fatherhood was not that uncommon. Historically, society agreed that a father had a right to be a forbidding "king of his castle." We're only a couple of generations removed from King George V's declaration that the father's proper role is to *frighten* his children. Even today, half of all Americans agree that "the father must be master of his own house."[2]

And in this traditional patriarchy, the father-son relationship has been one of dominance and submission, not of emotional connection. As a result, few of us had close, nurturing relationships with our fathers. Most of our fathers were either angry, rigid or emotionally distant — it was the time-honored way of keeping their place on top of the hierarchy.[3]

And the coldness or cruelty of that father-child relationship is reflected in the relationship we now maintain with our inner child. Many, if not most, men have a distant or a cruel relationship with themselves. The internal dialogue they have with themselves echoes childhood conversations with Dad.

Unfortunately, the lack of a nurturing father means that we've missed an important developmental stage. We never learned to internalize a kind parent — to incorporate his encouraging words into our own lifelong dialogue with self. *We never learned to be a kind father to ourselves.*

Instead we treat ourselves like objects, like machines. We criticize, pressure and drive ourselves, pound ourselves for our mistakes and shortcomings. When we meet disappointment or criticism in the world, we don't balance it with a friendly inner voice. Too often we attack ourselves.

I'm often shocked at how mean men can be when they talk about themselves. It's commonplace to hear men describe themselves harshly: "I am such a no good bastard;" "Really, I'm just a stupid sonofabitch."

As a young man told me, "I say things to myself that, if somebody else said it, I would punch him in the face."

Even the highly accomplished are not immune. For example, consider Bertrand Russell's description of the great Alfred North Whitehead:

> Like other men who lead extremely disciplined lives, he was liable to distressing soliloquies and when he thought he was alone, he would mutter abuse of himself for his supposed shortcomings.[4]

Many men regularly abuse themselves with such "distressing soliloquies." And as Mildred Newman has noted, a lifetime of such self-talk creates a kind of negative self-hypnosis.[5] You convince yourself that you're just not good enough.

Such habitual self-attack leads to despair, or to an obsessive search for diversion. According to Terrence Real, this cruelty to self is at the root of the covert depression that affects half of all men — it underlies the workaholism, alcoholism, sports and TV addictions, sex addiction, perfectionism, rageaholism and other addictions men use to escape from their painful inner lives. Real claims that for every depressed man he has ever treated, the man's relationship with himself has been a cruel one.[6]

Though common, this cruel relationship with self is mostly hidden. As I've mentioned, the harsh dialogue between my father and my inner child was invisible to me, even though it directed my life. And the cruel relationship is usually hidden from the world as well. It only occasionally breaks surface — when the man abuses himself aloud; publicly vents his anger at his son or wife; collapses from a stress-induced heart attack; or, in extreme cases like Richard Corey in the Simon and Garfunkel song, puts a gun to his head and kills the Inner Critic. But even when hidden, this remote relationship with self poisons the life of the man and his family.

A New Relationship with Self

Fortunately, I have discovered that I can change this cruel relationship with self. I've learned how to stop wounding myself. In fact, I've learned how to become my own best friend — that's much of what this book is about.

Creating a friendly relationship with self is absolutely key. For you can't live an authentic life until you create a healthy relationship with your inner self — until you know who you are and what you feel; until you value yourself and treat yourself with care and respect.[7]

As we'll see, in an ideal family parents model such a healthy relationship for their kids. Mirroring his parents' kindness, the child just naturally forms a friendship with his inner self. He becomes comfortable in his own skin. Such fortunate children go on to live rich, authentic lives.

But most men have not been so fortunate. We grew up in families where unhealthy patriarchal values dominated — including the idea that one must despise one's true self, and cover it with the Masculine Mask.

But it's not too late to change. Regardless of background, an adult can begin to create a friendly relationship with himself. By following a few simple principles, a man can actually become a Kind Father to himself. In doing so, he makes it safe for his real self to stop hiding and step out into the world. This way lies the joy of living a real life.

For me, the first step was to finally identify Dad's critical voice, and ask him to leave. In his stead, I began a daily discipline of speaking to myself with the same encouraging, nurturing, patient words that I try to use with my own children.

That decision to be a Kind Father to myself has transformed my life.

As you will see, it's not complicated. But it is revolutionary. As Terrence Real has written:

> A man willing to permanently alter the terms of his internal dialogue...seeks nothing less than a transformation in the way that he lives, the values he lives by. Such a journey goes beyond recovery. It is alchemy. It is a quest.[8]

3

The Quest:

Discovering the Kind Father

We are, in a sense, our own parents,
and we give birth to ourselves
by our own free choice of what is good.

— St. Gregory of Nyssa, 4th century

After the session with Neil, I set out to develop a Kind Father. I decide to create within myself a mentor who can give my inner child what my father didn't — encouragement, acceptance, appreciation and affection. And I begin to have a daily conversation with this new confidant.

In becoming a Kind Father to myself, I follow the advice of Bernard Berkowitz and Mildred Newman:

> The only way to true adulthood is through a real childhood.... Embrace the child in you, make friends with yourself....
>
> We can learn to be our own best friend. If we do, we have a friend for life. We can buoy ourselves up, give ourselves comfort and sustenance the times when there is no one else. We are our best source of encouragement and good advice. We are all accustomed to waiting for someone to give us a kind word, but we really have available to ourselves many kind words.[1]

I fashion my Kind Father from many parts, drawing on the
mentors I have known. For example, when I picture my
Kind Father I sometimes see Bill Cosby warmly encouraging
Theo, correcting him with kindly humor. Or Robert Young
of *Father Knows Best*, sitting on son Bud's bed, listening attentively, then giving thoughtful advice about a difficult situation. Sometimes he's Atticus Finch in *To Kill a Mockingbird*,
quietly teaching by principled example.

The Kind Father often has the reassuring voice and gentle
chuckle of Mr. Helms, the grandfatherly family friend who
engaged me in long conversations about trains and God when
I was eight years old:

> It was the day after my beloved older half-sister was taken
> away from our family by her natural mother. Despondent,
> I wandered off from Sunday dinner at the Helms' place and
> hid in their garden, sitting on the dirt in the corn patch,
> sobbing like a baby, hugging my black spaniel, Silky. After
> a long while, I heard the familiar jingle of Mr. Helms' keys,
> coming through the tall corn. Without a word to me, the
> old man slowly knelt and scratched Silky behind the ears
> for a long time. "Oh, you are a good dog, aren't you? You
> are just a fine dog, aren't you?"
>
> Finally he looked up at me, as if surprised I was there.
> "Son, this is such a fine dog — he must know some tricks?"
> Wiping away tears, I got up and showed him how Silky
> could roll over, sit up, shake-a-paw and play dead. Mr.
> Helms paid close attention, commenting on each trick in
> detail. At the end he scratched Silky's back, looked me in
> the eye and said, "Son, I admire the job you've done train-
> ing this fellow."
>
> After, we walked through the garden and back to the
> house, his hand lightly on my shoulder as he showed me
> a wooden train car he had just made in his shop. Just be-
> fore we went in, he patted me on the shoulder and smiled.

> "Calvin, God is going to take good care of Franny. And He'll take care of you." On the way home later that night, I was surprised to find the wooden car in my jacket pocket.

The Kind Father frequently has the gentle voice of my friend Chris, who speaks with wonderful patience and care as he teaches his son how to fix a bicycle brake. Sometimes the Kind Father has the voice of my brother Tom, an empathetic listener, who, hearing my latest troubles, murmurs "I'm sorry" gently over the phone, and draws the story out of me. In times of crisis the Kind Father switches to the gravelly voice of high school basketball Coach Millet — coolly drawing the play on the floor as we huddle around him in the last timeout of a frenzied, tied game.

The Kind Father sometimes has the voice of a confident mind — the voice of my English teacher Stan Boggs, passionately reading Shakespeare, then coolly analyzing the passage, parsing and weighing each word. "What exactly are 'the slings and arrows of outrageous fortune'?"

At other times the Kind Father has the reassuring good humor of counselor Peter McLean, who listens to my fears, leans back in his chair, hands behind his head, and encourages me to challenge those fears: "Always remember the Russian who complained on his hundredth birthday, 'Oh my, in my life, so many, many terrible, horrible, truly frightening things.... And some of them actually happened!'"

Paradoxically, the Kind Father has many elements of my mother, the child social worker. Two stand out. First, Mom responded to every adversity with a joke and a laugh. Some of our best laughs happened at the worst of times. Second, Mom had an "attitude of gratitude." On her death bed, she looked tenderly at her adult children gathered around, raised herself up and whispered these last words: *"There are so many things in the world to love, children. Look for them."*

And sometimes my Kind Father is a man that Mom taught

me about as a child — the carpenter from Nazareth who smiles at children on his lap; who cares for thieves, murderers, prostitutes, and me, even when I've failed; who tells me he loves me, that things will be OK, that good will prevail.

Surprisingly, the Kind Father even retains elements of my dad — his energy, his humor, and sense of adventure.

Taking a Walk with the Kind Father — The Conversation

You must also learn to talk to yourself. That's very important. You need to explain things, to reassure yourself. You need to establish an ongoing dialogue. It can help you through all kinds of tough situations.

— How to Be Your Own Best Friend[2]

It's early morning. I step outside the house, away from the rhythm of TV, radio, phone and family. I saunter down the hill towards the quiet beach, swinging my arms, and settling into the rhythm of my heart.

As my yellow lab runs ahead, sniffing and marking territory, I open myself to the sights, the sounds and the smells of a sun-drenched world. A chorus of songbirds is punctuated by the occasional melody of a red-winged blackbird. Down the forested hill, an eagle sits on the snag above the bay, scanning for salmon, as his partner rides thermals in circles above me. Over distant San Juan Island, the morning sun bursts from a thin band of molten gold clouds, and light begins to inch its way down the Douglas firs around me.

I casually check to see that there are no neighbors around, and then I begin my daily routine.

As usual, I picture a tall Kind Father walking beside me, his hand lightly resting on my shoulder. I don't really see him, but I am keenly aware of his hand on my shoulder and his warm regard for me. Today he's a bit like Mr. Helms, an avuncular late middle-aged man, speaking supportively to his adult son.

I give the Kind Father a voice. "How are you doing, Bud?" I ask myself aloud, softly. I try to speak to myself the way I try to speak to my kids — encouraging and nurturing.

With this single question, I feel my shoulders slump as I visibly relax. No matter how hard the last 24 hours, I am OK in this moment. I'm back to this safe place. It's OK now to feel whatever I've been feeling — sad, angry, afraid, whatever. I can express it all here and still be loved. This guy is on my side.

With the Kind Father's encouraging hand on my shoulder, I check in with myself:

"So, how are you doing? What are you feeling, Bud?"

I think about this question as I step off the road and onto the path to the beach.

Paying attention to my body, I shrug my shoulders, tilt my head first to one side, then the other. Slowly I answer. "Well, I've got this tightness in my shoulders, and my neck hurts. I'm feeling tense...a bit tired."

"So, what's happened since yesterday?"

I take a big breath, sigh. "Well, let's see...."

Suddenly a family of California quail skitters across the path and into the bushes, twittering. The mother makes a racket, heading into the bush by my feet, luring me away from her babies. "Wow!" I take a moment to follow the drama of the bird ostentatiously thrashing in the bush.

Then, returning from distraction, I think again about what I've been feeling. "Let me see...." I cast my mind back over the last day and pay attention to what I felt. "I've been feeling good about teaching the law students. I feel like I'm doing something positive for them. I appreciated their excitement about preparing that appeal...."

"And I liked the way I was with the girls. I got Nicole signed up for soccer, and that was good. I liked the fact I listened to Kristen's disappointment and didn't respond angrily.... M-m-m-m, and I felt good about getting Kathleen that book, I thought that was a thoughtful thing to do.... I really felt great about getting those tulip bulbs and planting them, and teaching Nicole something about gardening. That'll be a big positive for her, getting into planting things.... And I felt good about encouraging Rob, I respect myself for being faithful to a sick friend."

"But, right now," I sigh, "I think I'm feeling kind of low. I feel like I made a big mistake when I snapped at Kathleen to hurry up. I hurt her teenage feelings. I really feel bad about that."

The Kind Father is palpable, I can almost lean against him. Now the two of us are walking down the steep stairs to the beach, his hand still on my shoulder. He speaks, "You *were* giving her a hard time. But you didn't mean any harm."

I sigh again, surprised at how bad I feel about this. I hadn't realized how much the encounter with Kathleen had affected me. "Yeah, but she was really upset."

The Kind Father murmurs empathetically, "M-m-m-m-m. It sounds like it really shook you." He continues, "It'll pass. I just encourage you, next time, to take a little more time to listen to her. I suggest you take a big breath, slow down, and just let her explain.... I understand your frustration, but I encourage you to not raise your voice with her."

Relaxing a bit, I sigh again as the Kind Father continues, speaking in a warm, supportive voice.

"I want to encourage you to remember that your long-term relationship with her is more important than rushing to meet a deadline." Silence, as I ponder this. The Kind Father resumes, "But I really admire you for trying to change your old patterns. The time you're spending in listening to her will pay off big time. You two will work it through. I have confidence in you."

By now I'm on the beach. The gravel crunches under my feet. I walk over to the water's edge and pick up a flat stone. "What else, big guy?" The Kind Father asks.

"You know I am so sad about being separated from Deb and the kids. I miss them so much." I skip the stone across the water of the bay. Six skips.

"I really feel for you, Calvin. I know you're sad about being away from them. I know it's lonely. But I want to tell you how much I respect how 'present' you are for the kids. I respect the fact that you took them swimming yesterday, that you signed up Nicole for horseback riding, and that you're going to drive Kathleen to youth group." I am conscious of his supportive arm around my shoulders, as he continues.

"I know this is a really tough time, but I admire you for the way you hang in there for them. Somebody has to be the dad, and you're it. I really like the way you throw yourself into that. The kids will appreciate that some day."

We walk in silence. I'm aware of feeling encouraged. In the bay, a cormorant stretches up out of the water and flaps his wings to dry them. Then he dives, disappearing, water flattening over the ripple. Shortly the bird reappears, a silver fish in his beak.

I look around the beach and up at the fir trees along the bluff, where the eagle still sits, watching patiently. Finally, the Kind Father speaks again, quietly, "What else is going on?"

"Oh man, I'm worried about money. I don't know if I'm going to have enough to pay the mortgage this month."

"That's a big worry. It's gotta be hard." Now the cormorant flaps and takes off, first running on the water, then flying across the bay with his big wings extended, inches off the water.

"But you've been through this kind of tight situation many times before. You'll find a way through. Money is coming in from that contract. Or maybe from Joe. If necessary, you can borrow it. You can make do." He pauses. "I know it's tough, though.... What else?"

"I feel anxious about the court hearing. I don't know if I'm a good enough lawyer. I don't know if I can do it. It's an impossible case. The lawyer for the company is brilliant, Harvard Law and all that, and I don't know if I can compete."

I imagine the Kind Father giving my shoulder a playful squeeze. "You're a really good lawyer. Not the best, but good enough. You've done well in the past with tough cases. Hang in there, guy. Even if you're not perfect, I'll be pulling for you — even if you lose," he chuckles. "We'll talk about it afterwards."

Absentmindedly, I kick over a rock. Two tiny hermit crabs scramble in the hole, which rapidly fills with water.

The Father continues affectionately, "You know, you've got a lot of challenges in your life. This is a really tough hand you're playing. And you're managing to deal with it — not perfectly, but I admire the way you're managing. You're acting with integrity, not getting mad, and trying to do the best thing for the kids...."

I look out at the bay, then to my feet. I gently reach down and place the rock back over the tiny crabs. The Kind Father continues, "You're trying to do something useful with your career. You're not getting absorbed with yourself, and you're not drinking or drugging. I really like that, and I respect it. I want to support you in this. I admire the way you're living your life."

And so it goes. Basically, after I identify what I'm feeling, I try to talk to myself the way a supportive Father would. I express my encouragement, support, appreciation and respect.

The warm regard I express for myself is unconditional. I may express concerns about something I've done, particularly if it's contrary to my ethical view of things. But I don't give myself shit, I don't call myself names. I try to be loving and encouraging, even if I urge myself to do something different next time.

And when I'm done, I climb up onto the bald rocks overlooking St. Margaret's Bay. I look south to the distant snow-capped Olympic Mountains, and east to the yellow grassy hills and sandy cliffs of San Juan Island. Between me and the Island, the sun now glints the sea into a blinding quicksilver mirror, broken by a sailboat and freighter.

I thank God for the sky, the ocean, the eagles, the quail, the red-winged blackbirds, for my children, for each of my friends, the chance to practice environmental law in one of the most beautiful places on earth, the chance to teach and enjoy young people starting a legal career, the chance to play music, the ability to write, the opportunity to live in this beautiful place near the ocean. I give thanks for the joy in my life, and for the love my mother gave me.

I say the Lord's Prayer, and then I pray for my friends, family and people in need.

Afterward, I walk back up the hill to the house, refreshed. I'm ready for another day. Unlike the past, I am no longer divided against myself. I can devote myself wholeheartedly to the challenges of the day. I can approach my life with focused energy, calm confidence and a certain joy, even playfulness.

I've learned much on these walks. The Kind Father has taught me lessons that those who grew up in healthy homes learned naturally. He's taught me:

- I can make an existential choice to change the way I talk to myself. Instead of putting myself down, I can lift myself up. As the Jewish scholar Hillel said, "If I am not for myself, who will be for me?"
- It's OK to feel what I feel and think what I think. My feelings are important. I will pay attention to them, and accept them.
- Like every other person on the planet, I am worthy of love, encouragement and respect. I can provide these things to myself. And when I do, I feel great.

What Kind Parents Give Their Children

As the Kind Father parents me, I finally grow up with a healthy father — and start to enjoy the benefits of that healthy relationship. Let's take a moment to consider what a boy gains from a such a healthy, kind, non-patriarchal father. For this is the gift that I now give myself.

Emotionally mature parents raise their kids in what psychologist Robert Karen calls the "Country of Love." The parent has a friendly relationship with himself, and he passes it on, giving his child consistent warm regard. He speaks kindly to his children, is encouraging and responsive. He asks how they are doing, and listens with interest to the answer.

So when the fortunate child looks into the mirror of his parents' eyes, he sees a child worth loving. The child is consistently told that he is worthwhile — by his mother's admiring look, by his father's thoughtful attention to a toddler's persistent questions. If the child misbehaves, he is corrected, but the parents' underlying warm regard is always there, even during correction. As Karen puts it:

> Love is the umbrella, the overarching truth of this relationship, regardless of what else is felt or expressed.... We don't have to leave the Country of Love because of other things we feel....[3]

The love and acceptance of healthy parents is unconditional. The parents love the child for who he is — not for how he performs or appears. The child learns he has intrinsic value, simply because he's human and unique.

Healthy parents respect the child's boundaries, and encourage him to become his own person. Unlike parents that are absorbed with their own moods, healthy parents don't force the child to renounce his feelings and carry theirs. Because the parents have processed their own issues, they don't project their fear, anger and anguish onto the child. They don't pressure the child to reassure them, fill a hole in their hearts, or live out their unfulfilled dreams.[4] Instead, they encourage him to experience, express and manage his own feelings.

Healthy parents seek to guide, not control. Unlike patriarchs, they don't seek "power over" the child — but a relationship with him. And the relationship is a kind one. Perhaps the most important result is this: *Because the parents speak to the child with kind regard and encouragement, the child learns to speak to himself the same way.*

The child forms the habit of accepting himself, supporting himself. He sees his faults and understands the need to address them — but overall, like his parents, he holds himself in warm regard. He understands that his foibles and shortcomings are part of the human condition. He is fair and kind to himself, as well as others.

Since he likes and accepts himself, warts and all, he doesn't have to reject what he feels. He can be all the things he is, without shame. He doesn't have to wear a mask. He has the ultimate liberty — he can be himself. He allows himself to see what he sees, feel what he feels, and think what he thinks. He's comfortable in his own skin.

And because he accepts and loves himself, he avoids co-dependency. He need not depend on outsiders for a sense of worth, because he gives that to himself. Although distance and death may separate him from parents, he carries inside their steady encouragement and reassurance. As a result, he is not dependent on the praise of others, or frightened of their criticism. No matter what others say or do, he always has that inner resource. He can get hurt by others, but not devastated.

Thus, he doesn't have to control others and their feelings, in order to manage his own feelings. He can afford to let others have the freedom that he claims for himself — the freedom to experience his feelings, and be who he really is.

In sum, because his parents warmly accepted him, he accepts himself — and can live a free and self-actualized life.[5] Dr. Dorothy Nolte nailed it in her poem:

If children live with criticism,
  They learn to condemn
If children live with hostility,
  They learn to fight.
If children live with ridicule,
  They learn to feel shy.
If children live with shame,
  They learn to feel guilty.
If children live with encouragement,
  They learn confidence.
If children live with tolerance,
  They learn patience.
If children live with praise,
  They learn appreciation.
If children live with acceptance,
  They learn to love.
If children live with approval,
  They learn to like themselves.
If children live with honesty,
  They learn truthfulness.
If children live with security,
  They learn to have faith in
  themselves and in those about them.
If children live with friendliness,
  They learn the world is a nice place
  in which to live.[6]

The good news is that, even if we missed out in our original families, we get a second chance. For we can parent and encourage ourselves. We can become our own Kind Fathers.

Looking Inside

Go to your bosom, knock there
and ask your heart what it doth know.

— Shakespeare

The Tin Man — Our Story

One Spring a woodsman fell in love with a beautiful Munchkin girl. But the girl's bitter old mistress didn't want to lose her servant to marriage — so she paid the Wicked Witch to put a curse on the woodsman's axe.

Under the curse, when the woodsman swung his axe, the axe attacked his body. The next day when the woodsman began to cut down a tree, the axe cut off his right leg. Fortunately, the town tinsmith was able to fashion a replacement leg out of tin. The following day the axe cut off his left leg, but the tinsmith replaced it too.

Undeterred, and obsessed by his work, the woodsman returned again and again to the forest. One by one, he cut off his arms, and even his head — all were replaced by tin. He kept on working, while his flesh turned to cold metal.

But one day the enchanted axe attacked his chest and chopped out his heart. With the loss of his heart, the woodsman finally lost all memory of his true love. The one thing the tinsmith could not replace was the woodsman's heart.

And so work became the woodsman's whole life — all day long

the armored man strode through the deep forest, felling trees and chopping firewood. Methodically he turned the lush green woods into a field of stumps and earth.

Every day the work was the same. Yet, even if he had wanted to, the Tin Man dared not cry over his plight. Tears were a mortal threat — they would rust his joints, leave him paralyzed.

One day while cutting trees in the deep forest, he was caught in the rain, and rusted in place. For a year he stood immobile, stuck in a working pose, axe forever upraised.

Finally a straw man and a girl named Dorothy rescued the Tin Man. When he could talk again, his first complaint was:

"Bang on my chest.... It's empty.

The tinsmith forgot to give me a heart.... I'm all hollow!"

Dorothy and the straw man invited him to come with them to Emerald City, assuring him that the Great Wizard there could restore his missing heart. So the Tin Man joined the quest to see the Wizard.

When the friends finally met the Wizard, he promised that he would grant all their wishes if they killed the Wicked Witch. Enduring agonies and adventures, they accomplished this mission. They returned to the Wizard, and the Tin Man demanded his promised new heart. But the Wizard pointed out the obvious:

"Well, you've got a heart.

You've had it all the time!"

And when he really looked inside, the Tin Man saw that the Wizard was right. He cried when Dorothy left for Kansas — clearly he was still able to love. Miraculously, his heart had survived the axe after all. He had simply failed to see the heart that remained.[1]

As discussed in the last chapter, the Kind Father gave me freedom to explore my emotions. But all too often, when I looked inside, I was like the Tin Man — I simply couldn't see my heart. I still didn't know how to really look inside — how to pay attention to my inner life. Before I could do that, I would first have to unlearn patriarchy's ancient lessons.

Death of a Father — The Lesson

When I was 13 my father died while I slept.

The day before, I had come home from school to a hushed house. From the kitchen, I could see a glimpse of my parents' bedroom, Dad's massive body under a sheet, belly rising and falling with each labored breath. I could hear him murmuring to Mother, then she emerged, looking worried. "I'm going to buy him a bottle of vodka. I'll be right back," she muttered, rushing out the door.

This made no sense — she never bought him alcohol. Although he was an alcoholic, the stuff was never allowed in the house. He routinely hid his bottle from her — in the car trunk, in the toilet tank, under the porch.

Moments after she left, he called out in a raspy voice from the bedroom, "I need some water." I stood silent in the kitchen, pretending not to be there, afraid to move. Moments passed. "Tom...Calvin...Hey, somebody. Can I have some water?" I stood paralyzed. "I need water," he wheezed.

This disembodied voice was not the angry father I knew, the father I had always jumped to obey. Now, terrified of what I might find in the bedroom, I couldn't move. To my relief, my nine-year-old sister Candy rushed in, brushed by me, filled a glass of water and took it in.

An hour later, my brother David's wife came by and took the girls and me to stay overnight at their place. After dinner, we got a call that an ambulance had taken Dad to hospital. But things seemed normal. Diana drove us over to A&W, and we bought a gallon jug of root beer. We made floats and played Monopoly for a while. Then we went to bed. The girls went off to sleep with Diana, and I lay down under an army blanket on the living room couch. I fell asleep to the distant murmur of Diana praying with Candy.

At dawn, my teenage brother Tom shook me awake. When I startled, he hushed me. "Don't wake them," he hissed, pointing through the open door to where the girls still slept — Candy clinging to Diana's neck, Pam sprawled on the rug. He went over and closed the door. Turning back to me, he looked grave and whispered, "Hey, get up. We need to go for a walk."

"What?"

"It's important."

David, an ex-Marine, came inside and stood rigid at the front door: "Let's go, boys," he announced crisply. I looked up at David, but he refused to meet my eyes and looked away, jaw set. "Let's get out of here," he muttered.

I pulled on my pants and shoes, and scrambled outside after David and Tom. Still blinking with sleep, I struggled to keep pace with the 6'3" David, who purposefully strode ahead, heedless of us scrambling to keep up.

As we lagged behind, Tom fixed me with a serious look, grabbed me by the elbow and steered me to a halt against a large oak tree. Furrowing his brow, he looked me in the eye. I squinted in discomfort, marking how tired and washed-out Tom's blue eyes appeared in the harsh light of the rising sun. He raised his hand to shade his forehead, then softly announced, "I've got bad news."

I felt a chill up my spine.

Tom rushed on: "Dad died last night. He had a chest hemorrhage. He died at 2:30 this morning." Uncomprehending, I stared at him.

"Yeah," he whispered, nodding his head, "Yeah, he's dead."

I choked like I had a bone in my throat; and for a brief moment I cried. The emotion spurted out, in staccato gasps, like a fire hose with air in the line.

I was buffeted by bursts of feeling—shock and grief at the first death I had known; relief that the angry man was gone; guilt for having wished him dead; regret for not taking him a glass of water; pity for me, the fatherless child.

Gasping, almost retching, I stumbled down the sidewalk with Tom. When we got to the corner, David suddenly stopped, took a deep breath, and looked back at me. He braced his shoulders and spoke authoritatively, in his Marine voice, "We're the men in this family now, boys. We have to take this like men." He snapped the twig in his hands in two, and threw it to the ground. I noticed a slight tremor in his hand.

"We've got the girls to take care of. We all have a job to do," he said gruffly, looking away with slight disgust. I stood trembling, hiccupping sobs, hands rigid at my side — as ashamed of myself as if I was naked in the street.

David turned back to me. "Look," he said impatiently, "We've got to hold this together." He squeezed me on the shoulder, kind of a hard pinch. "Otherwise all hell breaks loose. Think about it — Dad would want you to be strong, champ."

He winked and gave me a thin-lipped smile. As my sobs subsided, his voice softened a bit. "Don't worry, Tom's the oldest now, so he's in charge. He'll take care of you." He slapped the dust off his hands, and strode quickly back to the house.

By the time David slammed the door, I had stopped crying. I didn't cry again — or mention my father — for 15 years.

A Hollow Man

Boy Code lessons like this taught me to bury my emotions — to hide them from others and myself. I learned it was dangerous to pay attention to what was actually going on inside. As a result, by the time I reached middle age I had no idea what I felt. When something upset me, I had only the vaguest sense of unease.

It's common. As Robert Bly has observed, most men do not notice their own suffering. A shadow falls between them and their pain. T. S. Eliot described it well:

We are the hollow men, we are the stuffed men....
Between the emotion

And the response
Falls the Shadow....[2]

We've been trained to not look at our hearts for any period of time. Instead, we've been told to turn our eyes away from our pain, and pretend it's not there. We've learned to ignore the feelings and *"get on with it."*

So when something impacted me emotionally — when the boss dumped on me, when I had an argument with my wife, when one of the kids disappointed, when my finances went south, when a neighbor died — I would feel upset for a moment. But then I would immediately divert myself from the feelings.

Like my brother David, I threw myself into the job at hand. I'd work long hours. Or I escaped into reading. Or I'd turn off the feeling by turning on the TV. Or I would compulsively recreate, taking the kids skating, biking, swimming...if that failed, I'd try to control my wife's behavior. Or I'd get angry.

But all these diversions had one compulsive motivation — to avoid relationship with self. I would do anything to avoid acknowledging that the person inside was hurting.[3]

It worked. Eventually I couldn't feel him at all.

Relearning How to Feel

I knew decades of numbness. But fortunately, in mid-life I relearned how to feel. It's not rocket science. I simply had to do two things: be a Kind Father to myself, and pay attention.

1. *Be a Kind Father to Myself*

Everything changed when the Kind Father taught me to have a friendly relationship with myself. By unconditionally loving me, he taught me to fully accept myself — all of myself — for the first time. As a result, I could finally stop running from prohibited feelings.

Like my brother David, the Harsh Father demanded that I censor out all my "unmanly" emotions. In contrast, the Kind

Father allowed me to feel fear, sadness, embarrassment, joy and ecstasy. For the first time, I began to experience all my feelings, not just the narrow range of feelings that the Boy Code allows.

2. *Pay Attention*

The other critical piece was to simply stop ignoring my feelings. I had to stop diverting myself with activity whenever I felt a vulnerable feeling. I had to break the compulsive habit of turning to TV, newspapers, entertainment, work, anger or control in order to distract me from myself. Clearing my mind of such distractions, I had to simply take a deep breath and pay attention to my feelings. I had to learn how to practice what Buddhists call "mindful attention."

To my surprise, once I learned to become a Kind Father to myself and pay attention, it was dead easy to be "in touch." I discovered that feeling one's self is a natural process — the unnatural process is suppressing it. If we just accept ourselves and remove distractions, the feelings happen. If we get out of the way, the heart will assert itself.

And the payoff is immediately gratifying. The moment I started to pay attention to my feelings, I began to see what lay behind the Male Mask. I began one of life's great adventures — getting to know my real self.

How I Pay Attention

To experience my feelings, I go for my morning walk with the Kind Father. First I slow down and pay attention. I take some time, and breathe deeply. Then I open myself up to feeling my body.

I try to feel the sensations in every part of my body, and ask myself where in my body am I feeling something? And what feeling is attached to that sensation? My body has much to tell me about what I'm feeling:

- Is that lump in my throat because I'm disappointed?
- My mouth is dry, is that anxiety?

- I'm feeling butterflies in my gut. What am I feeling?
- My jaw is clenched — am I tense?
- My face feels flushed. Am I angry?
- My palms and body are sweaty, am I feeling agitated?
- My heart is beating fast. Am I feeling afraid?
- I'm restless and can't sit still. What am I anxious about?
- Is that tightness in my neck connected to some feeling? What is it?

I try to pay attention to all my senses. As well as inner sensations, I pay attention to my surroundings. I look at the trees, sky and sea. I watch the gulls. I feel the breeze and the morning sun on my skin.

I take a deep breath, and then I:

'...go to my bosom, knock there and ask my heart what it doth know.'

That's what these morning walks are all about. My friend Chris often commences conversations with his sons with the friendly query, "How are you, buddy?" So as I walk along the water, the Kind Father leans over and asks me, "How are you doing, buddy?"

Then, like a parent in a healthy family, the Kind Father listens, while I ponder this question. "H-hm-m," I murmur, rolling my shoulders and gently stretching my neck muscles. "M-m-m." I consider what I am feeling right now.

I walk easily down the beach, with the Kind Father's arm lightly resting across my shoulders, taking my time to respond to his question. I relax, give time for my feelings to surface. I search my heart, and then speak the first thing that comes up:

"I'm sad about not seeing my kids enough...."

The Kind Father puts his arm around my shoulder, so I continue:

"I just hate being away from them this much.... This is so different from what I wanted my family life to be like...."

He responds by encouraging me, in a mature, reassuring voice:

"I know this is really hard for you, but I respect you for doing the best you can with it. I like the fact you see your kids as much as you can. I admire you for the effort you put into doing things with them, for taking Nicole frogging.... I really feel for you, buddy...."

We continue on in silence down the beach. Finally, the Kind Father asks again, "How are you doing otherwise?"

I pay careful attention to my response, as submerged feelings slowly float to the surface. One by one, they emerge, the flotsam and jetsam of the last few days. I give each feeling careful attention, try to identify and express it:

I feel worried about how I'm doing at work. I don't feel good enough...."

"I'm excited about L. I like her so much, but I'm not sure she likes me...."

"I was so embarrassed when John criticized me...."

The kind older man acknowledges each of my feelings, and goes on to support and encourage me — and to affirm my value as a person:

"I see you're worried, but I respect the effort you're making at work...."

"I want to acknowledge how brave it is for you to venture toward relationship again, after all the pain...."

"I really appreciate how you kept your cool when John criticized you...."

There's something about the process of describing my feelings to the Kind Father that clarifies them — and brings them to life. Feelings often remain vague until they are formulated and communicated to a listener, and the Kind Father plays this key role.[4]

And because he totally accepts me, I open my entire heart to him. As I reveal everything I feel, emotional deadness gives way to relief, tenderness, comfort, passion. Like a frozen river during spring breakup, the feelings begin to flow again.

Feeling is as natural as breathing once I pay attention, name the feeling, give myself permission and remove the diversions. But key to this process is my ability to actually *name* my feelings. And that's what men have forgotten how to do.

Retrieving My Heart — Finding the Words

Like most men, I didn't know enough words to accurately describe my feelings to myself. Trained by the Boy Code to not think about feelings, men — unlike women — lack a broad range of words to describe various emotions. This lack of emotional vocabulary is a real deficit — it's part of the reason that almost 80% of men have difficulty identifying what they are feeling.[5]

I knew when I was angry or feeling something quite powerful, but I didn't have the words for subtler feelings such as disappointment, discouragement, insecurity, irritation or the like. For example, if I was disappointed, I might not be able to accurately identify that feeling, because I didn't have the right word to describe it. Instead of telling myself I felt "disappointed," I would use words that either exaggerated the feeling ("I feel like crap"), or minimized it ("It's nothing — I'm just tired"). Or I would mistake the disappointed feeling for anger — the multi-purpose emotion which men tap when uncomfortable. As a result, I failed to experience the "disappointment" — because I was telling myself it was something else.

Before I could experience my true feelings, I first had to learn how to accurately describe them to myself — I had to learn an emotional vocabulary.

It's not difficult to enhance that vocabulary. As a starting point, there's a popular poster that shows a number of cartoon faces. Each face depicts a different emotion, described by a single word. Studying that poster helped give me more words for describing what is going on inside me. It taught me to consciously *practise* searching for the right word to describe my feelings. It's been very helpful.

On the following chart is a full palette of feeling words, with which I can paint a picture to myself of what I am experiencing. By consciously searching for the most accurate description of what I am feeling, I can learn to distinguish one shade of feeling from another. And I learn to describe to myself exactly what I'm feeling.

Canvassing this list helps me pinpoint exactly what it is I'm feeling. Clearly, it's a very different thing to feel "discouraged" than to feel "grief-stricken." It's a very different thing to feel "nervous" rather than "full of dread." Once I find the right word, I can tell the Kind Father exactly what's going on for me, and he can respond appropriately. At that point, I can empathize with myself — and with my precise situation.

As I reach for words to describe the feeling, I try to describe my feelings accurately and honestly — but also reasonably. I don't want to understate the feeling — but I don't want to exaggerate it either. I don't want to discount the feeling — and I don't want to inflate it. I choose my words deliberately, aware the words I use to describe an experience can actually shape the experience.

I want to feel the emotion — but I am aware that if I exaggerate the feeling, I make myself feel worse than necessary. I react differently if I say to myself:

> *"I am furious at T. for doing that."*
>   instead of
> *"I am irritated with T. for doing that."*

Naming Feelings: The Words

Happy

Content	Pleased	Satisfied	High	Up
Delighted	Ecstatic	Exuberant	Gleeful	Joyful
Jubilant	Radiant	Effervescent	Elated	Glad
Exhilarated	Intense	Enthusiastic	Merry	Lucky
Fortunate				

Angry

Mad	Frustrated	Furious	Irked	Outraged
Annoyed	Irritated	Disgusted	Displeased	Cranky
Cross	Disgusted	Exasperated	Fed up	Indignant
Miffed	Peeved	Ticked off	Vengeful	Vexed
Vindictive	Argumentative	Hateful	Hostile	Resentful
Aggravated	Belligerent	Offended	Agitated	Bitter
Fuming	Incensed	Livid	Sore	Wrathful

Excited

Ecstatic	Worked up	Eager	Enthusiastic	Fascinated
Thrilled	Volatile	Out of control	Beside myself	

Hate

Dislike	Bitterness	Loathing	Detest	Spiteful
Despise	Abominate			

Sad

Downhearted	Depressed	Unhappy	Distressed	Sorrowful
Discouraged	In the pits	Gloomy	Blue	Unhappy
Crestfallen	Grief-stricken	Dejected	Despairing	Forlorn
Dreary	Melancholy	Miserable	Mopey	Hurt
Pessimistic	Resigned	Somber	Torn up	Upset
Heartbroken	Mournful	Wounded	Wrecked	Tormented
Overwhelmed	Despondent	Anguished		

Surprised

Amazed	Shocked	Blown away	Overwhelmed	Alarmed
Bewildered	In turmoil	Incredulous	Paralyzed	Upset
Appalled	Astounded	Dazzled	Caught off guard	

Relieved

Change of pace	Comforted	Liberated	Lifted	Freed

Guilty

Wrong	Blamed	Accused	Sorry	Sheepish

Anxious

Worried	Fearful	Troubled	Bothered	Distressed
Concerned	Agitated	Uneasy	Edgy	Fidgety
Fragmented	Frenzied	Harried	Hysterical	Impatient
Intense	Irritable	Perturbed	Rushed	Stressed
Swamped	Impatient			

Hopeless

Discouraged	Insecure	Given up	Blocked	Powerless

Capable

Competent	Skillful	Bold	Prepared	Efficient
Inspired	Focused	Alert	Alive	Confident
Eager	Enthusiastic	Hopeful	Adventurous	Excited
Expectant				

Defensive

Protective	Guarded	Withdrawn	Avoiding	Ignoring
Resistant	Resentful			

Shamed

Embarrassed	Insulted	Ridiculed	Humiliated	Accused
Laughed at	Put down	Deflated	Guilty	Insecure
Mortified	Regretful	Useless		

Loving

Warm	Tender	Cherished	Important	Needed
Appreciative	Grateful	Thankful	Affectionate	Amorous
Compassionate	Devoted	Fond	Passionate	Endearing

Disappointed

Disturbed	Dissatisfied	Frustrated	Deluded	Defeated
Hurt	Failed	Rejected	Isolated	Left out
Excluded	Ignored	Unappreciated	Discouraged	Tense
Disheartened	Exhausted	Fatigued	Heavy	Listless
Weary	Disgruntled			

Comfortable

Calm	Soothed	Confident	Satisfied	Safe
Self-assured	Trusting	Contented	Mellow	Peaceful
Relieved	Serene	Tranquil	Playful	

Afraid

Apprehensive	Cautious	Full of Dread	Concerned	Frantic
Guarded	Terrorized	Anxious	Hesitant	Alarmed
In a cold sweat	Insecure	Jittery	Mistrusting	Nervous
On edge	Panicky	Suspicious	Wary	Worried
Uptight	Full of misgivings			

Confused

Ambivalent	Bewildered	Curious	Doubtful	Hesitant
Perplexed	Uncertain	Unclear	Undecided	Mixed-up
Disorderly	Confounded	Jumbled	Embarrassed	

Curious

Fascinated	Inquisitive	Interested	Intrigued	Yearning
Desirous	Hungry			

Detached

Aloof	Apathetic	Arrogant	Callous	Cold
Contemptuous	Critical	Disdainful	Bored	Grouchy
Indifferent	Judgmental	Nonchalant	Passive	Pitying
Prickly	Withdrawn			

There's a difference between saying:

> *"I am scared to death about facing this situation."*
> and
> *"I am feeling anxious about this situation."*

There's a difference between saying:

> *"I felt totally humiliated."*
> and
> *"I felt somewhat embarrassed."*

There's a difference between saying:

> *"I'm feeling all fucked up about this."*
> and
> *"I'm feeling confused about this."*

I just try to accurately, reasonably, and gently describe what is in my heart. The Kind Father gently helps me open my heart, without turning everything into a catastrophe.

Before, when I was chronically cut off from my feelings, I would tend to exaggerate feelings when they finally broke into my consciousness, in times of crisis. But now I try to avoid inflammatory words that overstate my feeling.

For example, in the past if someone hurt my feelings, I might say, "I feel like dying." Now, I'm more likely to say, "I'm feeling really blue." It's less bombastic — and more accurate. It recognizes the difference between a Big Feeling and Armageddon. I avoid alarming myself unnecessarily.

Similarly, when I identify that I'm feeling angry, I look a little further. Anger is generally a secondary emotion — an emotion that arises from underlying fear, sadness or anxiety. So I try to identify this underlying feeling. Instead of just saying "I am angry" I will try to get to the primary feeling by asking myself, "And under the anger, what am I feeling?" Usually the answer is "I am feeling sad," "I am feeling fearful," or "I am feeling embarrassed."[6]

Once I've identified the feeling, the work is almost done. Then I just have to give myself permission to feel it — to allow myself to experience the full natural force of the feeling. The key is to not censor any part of the feeling inside — to have courage to simply accept what is actually in my heart, and experience it. If it's sadness, I just acknowledge it. "Gee, that's really sad." And if tears come at that point, I welcome them.

So if I hear a sad song on the radio that triggers sadness about something in my life, I don't avoid the feeling. I may say to myself, "Gee, pay attention here, I think you could use a cry." And, unlike the days when it was decades between tears, I may actually choose to cry — put on a Ray Charles CD, allow myself to breathe freely and let the tears flow.

Conclusion: The Tin Man Rediscovers His Heart

Like the Tin Man, I never really lost my heart. I just had to pay attention to it. To recap, I was able to rediscover it by following a few simple steps:

- Hold myself in friendly regard (Be a Kind Father to myself).
- Pay attention to what I'm feeling.
- Identify the feeling with accurate words.
- Articulate the feeling to myself (i.e., to the Kind Father).
- Give myself permission and support to actually feel it, grieve it, if necessary.

The rewards of being in touch with my feelings are great. It's a relief to stop pretending — to stop running from unknown emotions. The simple truth is this: fully experiencing a hard emotion is actually far easier than trying to pretend it doesn't exist. Contrary to what I used to believe, I've discovered that I won't die if I cry. In fact, I feel refreshed after a cry — I feel stronger, and more able to meet life's challenges.[7]

For there's a vibrancy that comes from fully experiencing my real life — even sadness. As I explore my heart, I discover

that my life has a depth, a timbre, an authenticity to it that
it never had when I was "faking it." As I begin to honestly
accept my own feelings and self, I am keenly aware of my
imperfections. But I feel grounded and real. For the first time I
feel "comfortable in my own skin."

Psychologists tell us that getting to know your inner self
is a first step to living a self-actualized life.[8] I now understand
what they're talking about. As I get more in touch with my
real feelings, I am able to apply my heart more fully to my
endeavours, and to act in the world in an undivided and powerful way. I no longer waste mental energy on running from
my feelings, and pretending. I bring increased joy to my work,
my music and other activities.

In addition, I've discovered that paying regular attention
to small feelings keeps them from building to a crisis. I can
acknowledge them and deal with them when they are still a
manageable size. Feelings are no longer alien phenomena that
periodically overwhelm me. They are simply feelings — and
are both knowable and manageable.

Furthermore, intimacy with my own feelings prepares
me for intimacy with others. For I can't have an authentic
relationship with you until I know who I am. I can't possibly share myself with you until I know what it is I feel and
want. And I can't be comfortable with your feelings until I've
learned to be comfortable with my own. As Bernard Berkowitz observed:

> People can share whole worlds with each other, but first
> they must have access to their own.[9]

Knowing what I'm feeling has transformed the nature of my
intimate relationships. I am no longer just playing a role.
There's a depth and warmth, a comfort and confidence in just
being real about who I am and what I feel. There's a satisfaction in putting forward my real feelings to others — and being met by a real person in response.

Perhaps most important, the process of feeling things deeply and responding to those feelings with the Kind Father's compassion means that I finally have a real relationship with myself. My inner child is no longer an orphan.

Long ago, Socrates said that life's central challenge was to "Know thyself." More than a millennium later, St. Augustine pointed out the same thing:

> People travel to wonder at the height of mountains, at the huge waves of the sea, at the long courses of rivers, at the vast compass of the ocean, at the circular motion of the stars; and they pass by themselves without wondering.[10]

I will not spend a lifetime passing by myself without wondering. I will not ignore one of life's most important questions — Who am I? I will pay attention to my heart.

Speaking What I Feel

The weight of this sad time we must obey
Speak what we feel, not what we ought to say.

— Shakespeare

I soon discovered that identifying my feelings was not enough. I had to learn how to *share* them — to speak my feelings. Patriarchy has denied men this opportunity.

A Friend's Grief

The year I turned 12, John Higgins' wife died of cancer.

John and Dad were best friends — so when John arrived that night, the air was charged. There was a bit of awkwardness in the kitchen while Dad squeezed lemons for lemonade. "Hot enough for you today?" Dad asked.

"I guess," John smiled wanly, rubbing his unshaved face.

Dad leaned his full weight onto the lemon halves, twisting them on the nub of the glass juicer until the rinds were bare. "Yep, hotter n' hell. It hit 110," Dad said, as he stirred the frothy lemon juice into the pitcher. He shovelled the peels into the garbage and poured the lemonade. "Let's sit outside, it's cooling off out there now."

Making their way out to the dark porch, Dad and John sat on the old wooden chairs and lit up cigarettes. I hunkered down below them, on the porch steps. They sat silent for a long time, cigarettes glowing in the night, surrounded by the thick smell of honeysuckle and the throbbing of crickets.

John, usually garrulous, said nothing. Finally he stretched his lanky frame, sighed heavily, and stubbed out his cigarette on the plank deck. Dad took a drag, and stared down at his shoes. "I'm sorry about Mary, John."

"Thanks ..." John hesitated. "Thanks, Tom." He paused again, shaking his head as if dodging a mosquito. "It's OK now."

No one spoke. The sound of crickets broke like waves over our silence, engulfing us. Finally Dad shifted heavily on his chair. "It's a bitch." He took a swig of lemonade, and spat into the honeysuckle bush. Sitting back, he frowned, thoughtfully probing his ear with his little finger. "That Liston sure took Patterson by surprise."

John lifted his head and looked at Dad for a long moment. Finally he nodded. "Yeah, Patterson didn't know what hit him."

"Two minutes and six seconds. Jee-e-e-zus-s Christ! Half the people weren't even in their seats yet, and the fight was over," Dad said.

"Liston is a bull. Nobody can stop that guy," John said.

Dad spotted a mosquito on his knee, raised his hand, and then froze. "Patterson can." Swiftly swatting, he brushed the dead bug onto the ground, and smiled. "He's twice the boxer, and a whole lot smarter. He just got surprised, that's all. He wasn't even warmed up yet." Dad took another drink. "Over twelve rounds, he'd win."

"Uh-huh, probably," John murmured, pulling a big red checkered handkerchief out of his back pocket. He blew his nose, then cleared his throat long and loud before spitting it all into the honeysuckle bush.

"The big sunuvabitch just got lucky," Dad said. "He's no boxer — he's just a goddam hoodlum. They gotta have a rematch."

"You bet," John replied, absently. "No question about it." He leaned forward on the chair, to stuff the handkerchief back into his pocket.

With slow deliberation, Dad formed a fist with his right hand and contemplated it. "Damn, I'd like to see Marciano fight Liston. The Rock was better than both of 'em."

And so it went. When Dad got up to go to the bathroom, John and I were left alone on the porch. But John didn't tease me the way he usually did when we were by ourselves. Instead, we sat in silence, staring up at the stars. He seemed to be studying Orion, squinting hard, so I leaned way back and looked up into the Milky Way. After a while, John glanced over at me, as if to say something. But he just took a deep breath and looked down at his shoes, shoulders hunched.

Dad whistled softly as he came back through the kitchen, but at the front door he stopped and stared down at John's bent figure. A wince flitted across Dad's face. As he stepped out of the light and onto the dark porch, he awkwardly rifled his shirt pocket for a Camel. He lit it, then clapped a hand on John's bent shoulder, and offered the cigarette. "Here you go," he muttered gruffly. Then he lit one for himself and sat down heavily. In a few minutes they were talking about Yankee pitching.

At the end of the night, John went home to his motherless children.

After I went to bed, I could hear Dad puttering around for a long time in the kitchen. I could smell the smoke from his cigarette, saw the red glow in the dark kitchen. A couple of times he coughed, painfully. Later I heard the bedsprings creak as he got into bed. Mom said something, and Dad mumbled, "Poor bastard."

The next day John and Dad went on a bender.

The Wasteland

By ignoring the wound John had suffered, Dad and John played out the age-old male conversation. They reenacted the ancient story of the Knights of the Round Table:

Sir Percival goes on a quest to find the Holy Grail — the missing communion cup that Christ shared with disciples at the Last Supper, the same cup that later caught His blood at the Cross. For generations Knights have sought the Grail for its magic powers. It is said to heal the sick, and provide both endless food to the hungry and endless drink to the thirsty.

After many adventures, Sir Percival reaches a vast Wasteland. The land is sterile — crops fail, trees bear no fruit, women are barren. In this dead land he meets a King who stands motionless by a lake, fishing. Unknown to Percival, a terrible thigh wound has immobilized the King, so that he can do nothing but fish. And it is this same wound that created the Wasteland.

The Fisher King invites Percival to a banquet at the castle. During the dinner, the King is in agony from his wounds and must lie down next to the table. A procession of young men enters the banquet hall, led by one carrying a white lance which oozes blood. The blood is caught in a large cup held by another young man. Percival doesn't realize it, but this cup is actually the Holy Grail.

Percival longs to ask the King about his agony and about the bleeding lance. But he recalls that his mentor Sir Gornemant warned that a knight must rely on his deeds alone, and never "chatter." So the curious Percival says nothing.

When Sir Percival wakes up the next morning, he is alone in the Wasteland. The King and the castle have disappeared. Puzzled, Percival rides deeper into the barrens, where he meets a damsel who is cradling the body of a headless knight. Dropping the armored corpse, she leaps to her feet and shouts angrily at Percival. She demands to know why he didn't ask the King about his agony, and about the blood. She cries that if he had only asked, the King could have shared the cup with him — and broken the witch's spell. For the spell cannot be broken until men share the cup.

A single question to the wounded King would have healed the monarch — and restored the dying land. But because Percival had not asked about the blood, he had left the King in agony and the Kingdom a Wasteland.[1]

Like Percival and the King, modern men are trained to not speak our hearts. The rules of modern knighthood require us to not speak about our pain, or question the pain we see in others. As a result, we share the fate of the Fisher King — we conceal our private agony, and perpetuate a public wasteland.

John may have lost his wife and mother of his kids. I may be anguished by my separation from my family. You may be frightened because your daughter is anorexic. We may all be bleeding inside. But our conversation rambles on about the Super Bowl or the latest SUV. Behind our masks, we may be desperate. But to our friends we banter and speak of the Yankees.

We're brainwashed to be ashamed of our feelings — to believe that real men hide their wounds. The Boy Code taught us to never share grief, anxieties, fears or embarrassment. To do so would be unmanly. Instead, we hide our feelings, as we were taught in kindergarten. Big boys don't cry.

Long ago we were taught to emulate the modern knight, Superman. The Man of Steel stands unfazed, even as bullets bounce off his chest. He has a vulnerable side, but Superman's father warns Superman about the incredible danger of revealing the sensitive, human Clark Kent. He tells Superman that if he reveals his sensitive side, his enemies will have a way of getting at him where he is vulnerable. If he reveals himself, they will destroy him.

At some level, many of us still believe that emotional Kryptonite will get us. We fear that if we start showing our feelings, the grief will never stop, that we'll die. We don't realize the simple truth that we can go through feelings, experience them, share them and then move on, refreshed.

So when painful feelings arise, we pretend to be Men of Steel. We divert our attention from the tender feelings by obsessing on work, television, sex and sports; on cars, computers, hobbies, buying things or reading. We drink, we take drugs; we become angry, controlling or numb. We turn conversations away from painful topics. No matter what, we refuse to talk about what is bothering us.

This all comes at a cost. Paul Simon got it right in his classic song, *Sounds of Silence* — "Silence like a cancer grows." Our refusal to talk about our feelings contributes to our shortened lifespans, and our high rate of alcoholism, heart attacks, ulcers and suicides. It causes much of our depression and dysfunction.[2] And it turns our lives into fakery.

In this modern Wasteland, the Fisher King may be dying in agony and blood may spurt from nowhere — but still we sit in the vast banquet hall, and eat in silence.

There can be no healing until this silence ends.

Sharing Pain — Life's Sweet Secret

> *No bond*
> *in closer union knits two human hearts*
> *than fellowship in grief.*
>   — Robert Southey

Like most men, I was ashamed of speaking my pain. But I've discovered life's sweet, redeeming secret — a secret that many women know, but one that patriarchal society hides from men. The secret is this:

> Sharing my sorrow with others creates an unsuspected bridge from my heart to theirs. Simply by listening to each other, we can transform sorrow into something joyful — empathic connection. This connection is one of the greatest gifts that life offers.

I've discovered that my friends actually welcome it when I ask them to listen to what I'm going through. My courage to speak gives them the liberty to speak about what they feel. It allows them to drop the Masculine Mask, unburden themselves, and be real.

And deep down, everybody wants to be real.

As our masks drop, we see each other for the first time. Amazed, we discover how much we have in common. We recognize a fellow pilgrim on a path that we thought we traveled alone.

The fact is that we all experience loss — life is a "vale of tears." But loss carries seeds of blessing — it is life's best opportunity for meaningful relationship. When human beings share pain, they are at their best — most intimate, encouraging, noble, even joyous.

Christian wisdom recognizes this:

> Rejoice with them that do rejoice, and weep with them that weep...
>
> Have done with falsehood, and speak the truth to each other, for we belong to one another as parts of one body.[3]

And so does Buddhism:

> A woman who had lost her only child approached Buddha and asked for healing. He told her to bring him a mustard seed from a house that had not known sorrow. She went to all the houses in the world.
>
> Every house had known sorrow, but because they knew what pain felt like, they wanted to give her a gift to help her. She returned to Buddha and opened her heart to show him the gifts she had collected — understanding, compassion, acceptance, forbearance, courage, hope, truth, empathy, remembrance, strength, tenderness, wisdom and love.
>
> Buddha asked how she felt. She said, "Different. Heavier. Each gift comforts me, but I had to enlarge my heart to carry them all. What is this strange feeling?"
>
> "Sorrow."
>
> "You mean, I'm like the others now?"
>
> "Yes," said the Buddha. "You are no longer alone."[4]

Sharing sorrow brings us many gifts, including compassion. Most important, it brings us out of our inherent isolation — and into relationship with others. Without sorrow, we would continue to walk alone.

By refusing to talk about their pain, men have missed the whole point. The "strong, silent type" lives a lonely life. Sharing pain is not to be avoided — sharing both joy and pain is *necessary* if we want an honest connection with people and an authentic life.

> *I would that my life remain a tear and a smile...a tear to unite me with those of a broken heart; a smile to be a sign of my joy in existence.*[5]

Sharing the Cup

I've been lucky — I have found a place where I've learned to really listen to others, and to speak my feelings. Tonight I join six other men in the meeting room in a rundown building at the edge of downtown. We sit in a circle, gabbing about cars, until the husband and wife who facilitate the group come in. After a moment of meditation, we begin.

The Failure to Listen

We don't speak — but we don't listen either. We don't know how to listen so that our friend can speak from the heart. Instead, like Dad, we hand the new widower a cigarette and start talking baseball.

Hemingway had it right — "Most people never listen." In most conversations, instead of listening to you, I'm focused on what I'm going to say in response. Or I interrupt you, so that I can talk about what's really on my mind. Or I'm thinking about something else altogether (Did I leave that tool in the garage?), while I nod my head. Or I give you an anodyne ("It will all be OK...."), because I don't want to feel your pain.

When listening is painful, I may cut off your story and lecture at you. Or preach at you. I may shut you down by being emotionally unresponsive. Or I may get picky and correct you, or interrogate you ("What did you do to make him so mean?").

Alternatively, I may go intellectual on you — and spend my time interpreting and analyzing what you said, instead of simply listening. Or I may put a label on you. ("You sexist! You wuss!") Sometimes I'll devalue what you've said by "one-upping" you. ("Your mother died? Well, both my mother and father died last year.")

This men's group grew out of an anger management group, and has continued for about 15 years. Seven men get together weekly for a two-and-a-half-hour gathering where we "check-in" with each other. We take turns simply sharing what has gone on in our lives in the last week — the tough stuff, as well as the good.

One at a time, we take turns speaking. When one man is speaking, no one else interrupts. The idea is for that man to get in touch with his experiences and feelings, and speak of them. For the listener, the idea is to give full attention, and only give feedback afterward, if invited. The listeners' major role is to bear witness, not to give advice.

This is a place where I can come and be completely honest with myself and my friends. Much of what I know about myself I have learned in this room, from the other men, from the woman who co-facilitates along with her husband — and from listening to myself as I try to figure out my life.

Frequently, I'll abandon listening altogether and just respond with straight advice: "I think you should divorce her;" or "Why don't you just give him an ultimatum on his drinking?;" or "I would just take away my son's privileges if he did that;" or "You should see my psychologist." Instead of giving my heart, I give a solution. Although sharing one's experience can sometimes be useful, giving advice often cuts off real listening. It can be used to avoid the pain of really hearing the other's hurt.

Gratuitous advice can undermine the recipient, implying they're not competent to figure the situation out. It confuses the person, who often gets contradictory advice from different people. And it ignores the fact that each person is *the expert* on their own circumstances.

In a multitude of ways, I abandon my duty to listen with empathy. I forget Scott Peck's profound wisdom:

> More often than not, the most healing thing that we can do with someone who is in pain, rather than trying to get rid of that pain, is to sit there and be willing to share it.[6]

Patrick begins. A tall, athletic, greying man, he shifts in his seat.

"It's been a hard week. As usual, Jill was sick again this week. She was in bed all week. So I was in charge of the four kids, plus trying to work." He pauses, nods his head thoughtfully, and looks at the ceiling. The rest of us just sit, quiet and attentive.

"Tuesday was the worst day. I was feeling rundown, headachy, a bit achy all over. And I got flak from a manager over a report we've had some delays on. No big deal, but he was overly critical, I thought. So work wasn't good, and I had to stay late to deal with it." He sighs.

"Then I rushed home to deal with dinner stuff, and getting the kids to bed. So I was just racing around.... Then I got a phone call from my mother, and she was stressed out, because she's dealing with moving...."

"Then it's eight o'clock, and I still haven't had a chance to just sit down for a minute and relax. But now it's time to put the boys to bed. And we get in their room, and the bed is broken.... And I ca-n-n-nt believe it!" He rolls his eyes in mock disbelief. With a taut grin he raises his hands in a gesture of surrender.

"The slat under the box spring had fallen out. They'd been jumping on it. I have told them a hundred times not to jump on it, but they had gone ahead and broken it. Geez, I was really frustrated, and I let them know it. I raised my voice and said, 'It's like a bunch of animals in here. I'm really, *really* disappointed in you guys. I'm going out for ten minutes. When I get back, this BETTER BE FIXED!'"

He sighs and slowly shakes his head back and forth. "And that's when Billy started to cry...." He frowns and looks at the window. "That was tough. Geez, I suddenly realized that I had really scared him. I felt so bad. The one thing I don't want to do with my kids is what my father did to me.... I still remember how scary that was, having an adult four times my size yelling at me." He bites his lip, then looks around the room, taking a moment to look each man in the eye.

"So I sat down beside him and apologized. I asked him if I'd scared him, and he said yes...." He pauses again and stares at the floor. "Geez, that is hard to hear." Again there's silence in the room. It's as if Patrick is having an intense conversation with himself; we are just witnesses. Then he looks up.

"But I sat down with him on my lap and talked to him until he calmed down. Later I read him an Asterix book, which was fun — he really enjoyed that.... Still, I wish I hadn't snapped at them. I really have to do a better job of that."

There's a long silence, but there's no awkwardness in the room. This is Patrick's time, and there's no rush. Patrick absently rubs his chin and looks at the ceiling, contemplative. "Let's see, what else. Jill has been sick all week, so I didn't see much of her. She's just been in bed all week, and I find that lonely, frankly. I don't like it at all."

"She just sits in front of the TV. On Wednesday after I finished washing the dinner dishes, I went in and tried to start a conversation with her — and she snapped at me. She said I was interrupting her show." He gestures in disbelief, palms out. "I mean, she's been watching for six hours straight, but *I'm interrupting?* That was hard to hear. I could feel myself getting angry, so I took a time out, and I went down to my shop and worked on my bike."

Silence. He clears his throat softly. "Overall, I guess I'm feeling tired. It's a lot of work, with dishes, the kids, getting to work and all.... I feel like I'm doing it all." He pauses for a long time. "Other than the incident with the boys, I'm not concerned about any of my behavior. But I feel bad about the boys."

He looks at the ceiling again, shrugs his shoulders. "I'm done. That's all for me."

John, a tall, retired teacher with craggy good looks, sighs.

"M-m-m-m. Whew." He slowly exhales, empathetically. "Would you like some feedback?"

Patrick nods, "Sure."

"I imagine myself being Billy, having you stand over me and shout. And I can imagine that would have been pretty darn scary." Patrick nods soberly. "I mean, this huge guy looms over me, shouting REALLY loud, red-faced and looking pissed off. It makes me think of my dad. I feel scared just hearing you describe it."

Patrick nods and is quiet for a long time. No one jumps in to fill the hole of silence. Finally, he nods again, "Yeah, I see what you mean."

Don, a husky, ruddy, 45-year-old construction contractor with thinning hair, clears his throat. Then he speaks up. "I agree. But it was good work in catching yourself and apologizing to your son. I know you feel bad about making Billy cry, but I think you're giving Billy a freedom your dad never gave you. You've given him the freedom to say 'ouch', and know that you'll pay attention to it.... That's real progress, and I really respect that."

Don pauses, allows the silence to fall again. "Geez," he shakes his head and clears his throat. "I just see how difficult life is for you, day after day. I try to imagine myself in your situation, and I don't think I could do it. Look at it...." He enumerates his points, finger by finger: "Going to work, taking care of four kids, cooking the dinner, keeping up with the house, looking after your mom. You have a really tough situation. I really respect how hard you work at it, the way you keep pitching."

Brian, a rotund young Jewish man with an open, cherubic face, nods. "I agree. Tough road."

Patrick nods in return, quiet, eyes glistening.

Don continues, "And I have a ton of respect for you meeting those challenges. Those kids are lucky to have you, and to have you trying to change."

John passes around a package of gum. Everyone takes one, except me. I'm next.

My turn. Before the meeting I have prepared for this moment by thinking about what happened over the last week — how I felt about it and how I might speak about it. In addition, things people have said tonight have triggered feelings for me. I speak:

"Well, my back hurts and I'm feeling a bit tense." I pause. It's quiet, but no one rushes in to say anything. They wait attentively to hear from me.

"I guess overall there's good and bad this week. Work is going really well. I did a really good job on this murrelet case, and I got some encouraging comments from my boss."

I breathe deeply. "But, I'm feeling lonely. I'm really missing my kids — missing not seeing them every night. I try to see them every day, but it's really hard. Like, I'll go by and wait outside Deb's place, and sometimes I'm waiting a long time for Nikki or Kristen to come out, and I feel like a real outsider...."

"I miss the comfort of us all being together in one house, one sanctuary. I miss the house, you know, it was such a beautiful place by the water, and had all the trees and bushes I'd planted. I feel a real loss about selling it, and living in this small, poor place where I am now. And now there's so much tension between Deb and me. Like, I'll be going off with Nikki, and Deb will speak to me, but it's about how much money I should pay her.... So I get really sarcastic with her about that, and that doesn't go anywhere good...."

"On Monday I took Nikki to soccer, but she was upset and hung back and wouldn't play, and I felt embarrassed, thinking people will blame me for being a bad parent. So that was tough."

"Let me see, what else is going on for me?" I sigh and am quiet for a while. "Oh-h-h-h, I had an embarrassing moment with Helen. You know I really like her. I'm kind of smitten. So we went to dinner, and had this great talk. Like, I really love talking to her, we're on the same wavelength. It's quite neat. And so the next day I sent her an e-mail about how much I liked our talk, and I said I thought she looked beautiful in the sunlight in the restaurant. And she wrote back, saying that made her uncomfortable, that wasn't the kind of relationship she wanted. And I felt really embarrassed. Man, I felt bad, not good enough. It really bummed me out for a couple of days. I felt old, unwanted, fat...." I pause. "But I just really like her, even if it is as a friend."

Silence. Nick, a carpenter who resembles a middle-aged Paul Newman, sighs and gives me a sympathetic look.

"And there was some really good stuff this week too. On Sunday I took Nikki swimming, and we had a great time with her friend. And on Tuesday, she phones me up and says she wants to catch a snake. So we get a cardboard box, and go off to Lochside, where we heard there were snakes. So for an hour we're wandering around in this field, kicking at the grass, looking under rocks and logs. And we don't see anything, so after an hour we're about to go, when we walk by this big piece of black tarpaper that's lying on the grass. Nikki says, 'Dad, do you think there are snakes there?' And I shrug and say no. But she lifts it up and there's a *whole nest* of garter snakes, a whole bunch of snakes writhing around.... And now the girls are screaming and Nikki is saying 'Get one, Dad, get one!'"

The men laugh. Nick shivers involuntarily, and slaps his knee. "Ar-r-gg-gh! Picking up a snake!"

I continue. "And of course I'm scared, because I don't like snakes. I grew up in rattlesnake country, where we hated them. So, I've never picked up a snake, but Nikki's shouting, 'Get it Dad. Get it! It's going to get away, DAD!' So I just take a big breath, reach down there and grab it. This great big fat one, it was pregnant so it hadn't gotten away. So that was really cool, because now she's got this pet she caught...."

"That's great," John interjects, as Don grins at me.

"Then an hour later, the snake barfed up a slug — that's why it was so fat." This is greeted by revulsion and laughter.

I stop and wait for quiet, then continue. "So, there's a lot of challenges in my life. But some good stuff too. And I'm glad to be here. No matter how tough the week, I say to myself, 'you can always make it to Thursday night.'"

I pause, and check inside to see if there's more to report. "OK. I'm finished."

Nick speaks up softly. "Do you want feedback?" I nod.

"I know this is a tough time for you. When I was separated from my kids, whew! Man oh man, I've been there." He catches my eye, and continues kindly, "I know how bad it can get. But it gets better. Things are so much better for me and my kids than I'd ever dreamed they could be." He smiles warmly, "Hang in there. Give me a call anytime. You've got my number."

Patrick speaks. "I've got a lot of respect for your dedication to your kids. The fact is, I don't know anybody more dedicated to their kids. You really do a lot of fun stuff with them. Every week you're in here talking about canoeing, shrimping, frogging, catching newts or some kind of adventure. You make the time for them. That'll pay off in the end. They'll remember that."

"Thanks," I say, looking around at the circle. Don and Patrick smile. The others nod, warm, accepting.

When I first came to this group, this warmth surprised me. After sharing some of the bad stuff in my life, I expected criticism, perhaps repugnance. But when I looked up from the embarrassment of telling my story that first meeting, I was startled by the brotherly warmth and affection in their eyes.

Martin Buber described this gift:

The most precious gift that one human being can give to another is the presence that empathy requires.[7]

This group has changed my relationship with men. Before, I mistrusted men and feared showing them my emotions. My intimate friends were always women. But by coming to this group — and by becoming a Kind Father to myself — I have finally learned that there are men that I can trust.

Now it's Don's turn. He clears his throat and speaks. "I feel I'm being unfair with Bev. Before we started going out steady, I was always trying to impress her — I was always on my best behavior. But now she's really *gone* for me, like she really, really likes me. And I feel myself getting more and more distant." He stops and clears his throat again.

"It's like I'm stepping back from her. So, on Saturday I feel like I really treated her badly." He shifts in his seat and again clears his throat. "We were in the hot tub and she said something about the way I treated my brother when he came into the office the other day...."

"And I got mad and I cut her off. I just stopped talking to her. So I just get out of the tub and went to the other room, and I just freeze her out. She's saying like, 'What's wrong? what's going on?' and I said nothing, just nothing. And she's following me around, saying, 'What is it? What did I do?'"

"But I'm *just pissed*." With an awkward grin he looks around the circle, shaking his head in disapproval. "I just go into the bathroom and lock the door." He looks into the distance to recapture the moment, and takes a deep breath.

"And I just turned her off. Here she's really unhappy, trying to make it right for me, but I'm just not buying it, I'm not budging.... I just go in the kitchen and ignore her." He leans over and looks at the floor, then looks up, grinning weakly, shaking his head. "That's what I do. I do it all the time, I've done this with other women. Like the closer she gets to me, the colder I get...."

"Damn, I hate this. I can feel the power imbalance, and I don't like it. I know it's unfair of me, and I don't want to do it anymore. I don't want it to be like my other relationships.

I really care for her. And that's not what I want." He looks at Candy, the co-facilitator. "That's what I've always done, and I want to change that."

He clears his throat. "So I've made an appointment to see a counselor to talk about this, because Bev doesn't deserve this. This is my issue. She deserves better. And I want this group to hold me accountable on this. If I backslide on this, I want you to call me on it."

He wipes his forehead with the back of his hand, and looks around the circle. "I'm finished."

Candy, the co-facilitator, responds. "You want feedback?"

"Sure."

"Well," Candy leans back in her chair and looks at the ceiling thoughtfully. "I think I understand why Bev would feel bad. If I were her, I'd feel punished. Like, I've just said this one thing that I didn't mean to be hurtful, and now you're refusing to talk to me. I would find that really hard."

Brian speaks up. "Yeah, I can see how tough that would be for Bev."

John leans forward. "I see what Candy is saying too. But I was just sitting here thinking about how far you've come, Don. I respect you for being so honest with yourself. You realize that distancing your partner is a problem, and you're trying to fix it. And I respect your being accountable for poor behavior, and committing to change it. I think it's really exciting to see you go through those changes, to see you working to build an authentic relationship with Bev. It's exciting to watch."

And so it goes — hurts, hopes, and gladness all come out as we talk about what's really happening in our lives. There's a lot of laughter. There's support, brotherly affection. Periodically there's a sympathetic sigh as one of us recognizes a scene from his own life in the other's story. At the end of the night, we hug each other, and part with a few joking, friendly words.

After the meeting, I feel in touch with myself, connected to friends, part of an accepting community. It's a privilege to gather in this place with friends who want to live real lives, not "pretend" ones. It's a privilege to share my life with them. I go home with my friends' kind words in my ears — words that I often call back and use when I'm being a Kind Father to myself.

I'm likely to spend the rest of my life meeting with these friends on Thursday nights. I just wish that Dad had had a place like this. It might have turned out better for him, and for our family.

The Importance of Mindful Listening

The main reason the group works is because of a few simple rules that we follow. The most important one is that we don't interrupt a man during his turn to talk. We listen without crosstalking.

In addition, we don't try to fix each other's problems, or rescue each other. We generally avoid giving advice. We just listen. We have learned to listen with the key elements of "mindful loving" that David Richo has identified:

- attention
- acceptance,
- appreciation and
- affection[8]

For there's something healing about simply being listened to with attention and appreciation. This is likely the reason why Confession was a universal religious tradition — it was the one place where a person was *listened to* intently. A person who felt isolated, who didn't feel heard by his boss, family or friends could go to Confession — and know that he could speak his heart to someone who would pay careful attention.

Indeed, as we listen to each other in the men's group, it sometimes feels like a sacred communion, like we're sharing the Grail. When a member of the group talks about what he's feeling, the rest of us listen intently. You could hear a pin drop, as we bear witness to his pain, confusion, joy.

Although we avoid being co-dependent and taking responsibility for the man who is speaking and his problems, we try to fully acknowledge his experience. We give close attention to his pain. As he speaks his truth, we listen in the true sense of *com passion* — we "feel with" him. If he's close to tears, it's more than likely that one of us will be too. For as I acknowledge his feelings, I somehow become more aware of mine. If he articulates an emotion I have suppressed, the emotion comes alive within me.

Then, when it's my turn to be heard, I explain what I'm feeling, what I'm going through. And in explaining it to listeners, I explain it to myself. To make them understand, I really have to go inside and carefully examine what's there. As I speak, I discover and clarify my own feelings.

In the end, these attentive friends provide an invaluable mirror. When I finish talking, and look up at my friends' faces, I see a reflection of my life. For example, a circle of sad, concerned faces makes me drop my denial that things are bad. At such times I realize I'm in a sad spot — but not alone. I'm sharing a healing cup with my friends.

The first duty of love is to listen.[9]

Taking it to the Streets

I've extended what I've learned in the group to my daily life. For example, I've developed a network of friends I can phone when I'm upset.

This grew out of necessity. After my marriage broke down, I found myself adrift, in the greatest crisis of my life with little emotional support. At the same time, through counseling, reading and my men's group, I was becoming more aware of my Inner Life, and the need to share it. So I made a deliberate decision to develop a network of people that I could talk to about what was going on in my turbulent life.

I asked my brother, members of the men's group and a handful of trustworthy people: "Can I call you about stuff, when I'm having a hard time? Sometimes things are really crazy, and I just need someone to touch base with, in the middle of the crisis. Can I call you for a few minutes when things get hard?"

The result has been gratifying. I have learned if I phone a friend right away and share my feelings ("She said_____, and I just feel so discouraged."), that the stress dissipates.

Usually, it doesn't take long to debrief. "This happened. That happened. I felt bad (or sad, embarrassed, overwhelmed, anxious)." I'll often talk just long enough to recognize what has just happened to me. I am not soliciting advice, but a moment of witness. I'll say to my friend, "Hey, I'm having a hard time here. I'm not looking to you to fix it or make it

The Courage to Listen

As I've learned to listen, I've begun to appreciate the importance of courage in relationships. For sometimes what keeps me from listening is a lack of courage. I find myself *afraid* to listen to a person who is angry or disappointed with me.

This is why I failed to hear my family's sadness and anger for many years. My self esteem was so low, I would not allow dissatisfaction to be expressed to me — it was too threatening. Instead, I'd try to *change* their feelings. For example, if my daughter was unhappy because of the way I'd talked to her about chores, I would try to "jolly" her out of her mood. I would look for ways

to entertain her, distract her, to cheer her up.

If that didn't work, I would try to talk her out of her feelings. "That wasn't really so bad. How would you like it if I treated you like Karen's dad does? He makes her do the lawn every week, and he's not as nice as I am about it...."

Finally, if she didn't abandon her feelings, I would get angry and demand that she shut down her expression of feelings. "Damn it, let's move on. Life is calling out there...."

But I've learned a different approach. I've learned to screw up my courage and simply allow the person to express their anger and better, but I want you to know this is hard. I just need to get this off my chest."

Once I do that, the problem is now *out on the table*, instead of festering inside me. After debriefing, I share a laugh or occasionally a tear; and receive warm attention, acceptance and support from the other end of the phone. I soon go back to my life clear.

There are a number of benefits:

- When my friend listens to me, I can figure out what I'm really feeling.
- I acknowledge a troubling event, put it in perspective, and "clear" it quickly. This keeps me from being distracted by it for the rest of the day — or blowing up later. The proverb is right — shared sorrow is half sorrow.
- If I'm having a disagreement with someone, phoning a third party gives me a chance to take a "time out" and get grounded. I avoid digging in deeper with the first person.

---

disappointment — to allow them to tell me what they really feel.

Frankly, it's still scary for me. But I've discovered that I can survive the painful feelings, acknowledge them, apologize if appropriate, and move on. And I've discovered that once the other person has their say and I have heard their grievance, the healing and good will can begin in a way it wouldn't have, if I had cut them off.

To my surprise, some of my most satisfying, intimate conversations have started with a person expressing their unhappiness with me — and me really listening and responding.

But first I must have the courage to hear the other's negative feelings. Fortunately, the Kind Father has given me this courage. Bolstered by his encouragement and acceptance, I no longer depend solely on what others say to gauge my worth. As a result, I can allow people the freedom to express their feelings, including displeasure.

The payoff is that if I am brave enough to allow you to be real with me, I get to meet the *real you* for the first time. We drop the charade. Openness and courage lead to real intimacy.

- By expressing my feelings, I realize they are just that, Big Feelings, not the end of the world. Then I move on.
- I'm protecting my health. Studies indicate that sharing with friends reduces stress and cardiac risk. [10] One reason that Okinawans live longer than virtually anyone else on earth is that their culture encourages them to meet regularly in mutual support groups. [11]

Of course, my friends may not be available when I call. The first thing I do is ask if they can spare a few minutes. "Hey, Steve, I'm having a hard time, have you got five or ten minutes?" If they're busy, I move on. No one individual is totally responsible for me. That's why I have a list of people to call, and I go to the next person on the list.

In the past, I would have hesitated to call people like this. I would have feared being an imposition, and my pride would not have allowed it. But, to my surprise, I have discovered that my friends welcome my calls if they're not busy. They know I am not wasting their time, that I'm phoning about something important.

Our friendships have deepened. Now they phone me when something tough happens to them. We are learning to bear witness to each others' lives.

Conclusion

The person who tries to live alone
will not succeed as a human being.
His heart withers if it does not answer
another heart. [12]

It's decades now since Dad and John Higgins went to their solitary graves. I don't want to die like Dad, unable to tell my best friend the truth about my life. I don't want to be an actor, working from a macho script. I am determined to speak my own truth, and live my own life. I will claim the energy, the joy and relationship that come when I stop hiding my interior life as if it were shameful.

For the fact is, I don't walk through the Wasteland alone. I'm surrounded by fellow pilgrims who face the same challenges I do. Sir Gornemant was wrong — we don't discover the Holy Grail with heroic deeds and manly silence. We discover the Grail when we turn to our brothers, look them in the eye and share the cup. This is life's greatest gift.

So I will not ignore it when my friend the Fisher King lies in agony, or when blood appears from nowhere. I will speak when it hurts; I will listen when my friend hurts. We will share our hearts.

And when we share, the quest for the Holy Grail is finally completed. My wounds heal; the bleeding stops. The Wasteland blooms, rivers run clear, crops ripen. It is springtime in the Kingdom.

I am surprised by joy.

Anger: Escape from Feeling

Real men cry bullets, not tears.
— William Pollack

During the last hunt, the mammoth white whale had turned on Captain Ahab and devoured his leg. Ahab now walks on a peg leg made from a whale jawbone. With this ivory leg, and a scar that runs from scalp to coat collar, Ahab looks wounded from head to foot.

The angry captain collects a menacing new crew, and demands that they drink an oath to kill Moby Dick. They set sail for revenge, tracking the white whale across the world's great oceans.

Meeting another ship, Ahab asks the captain if he's seen Moby Dick. Without a word, the man holds out his right arm — from the elbow down it, too, is bare whale bone. Undeterred, Ahab furiously orders his ship forward. Demanding blood from his crew, he uses the human blood to temper a new harpoon in the forge. He vows to personally sink the blooded harpoon into his foe.

One night a lightning storm strikes and fire dances ominously around the ship. Fearing this omen, the crew begs the captain to abandon the hunt. But a defiant Ahab stands at the foot of the blazing mast, and angrily vows to destroy the whale.

In the Sea of Japan, Ahab comes upon another ship. The ship's desperate captain asks Ahab to help look for the man's 12-year-old son, who's just disappeared in a small boat. But Ahab refuses — he's heard that Moby Dick is nearby.

At last, Ahab confronts Moby Dick, and a long battle ensues between whale and men. Over three days, the beast kills crew members
and destroys small whaling boats. But Ahab persists. And when the
whale turns to ram the main ship, Ahab angrily hurls the harpoon.
The blood-tempered shaft sinks into the whale, and Ahab's ven-
geance is complete.

But as the wounded whale dives to the ocean floor, the harpoon
rope sings, tightens and catches the captain by the neck. Moby Dick
drags Ahab, his ship and his entire crew to a watery grave.[1]

Anger dragged my dad — like Ahab — to a tragic and lonely
death. In his last years, Dad was furious with the world. Living with him was a lot like serving on Ahab's ship. However, I
have recently come to understand Dad's fury, his wounds and
his own doomed voyage.

My Dad's Anger

On a brutally hot day when I was eleven, Dad took us out for a
late afternoon swim. It was a long drive down a dirt road, through
bleached grasslands and dusty orchards. When we reached the irri-
gation canal, Dad geared the old Ford down, inched onto the tim-
ber bridge and stopped. The dust plume that had been following us
caught up and poured through the car windows.

Opening the doors, Tom and I stepped out onto the timbers. For
a minute we stood and looked down at the rushing, muddy water.
"Last one in is a rotten egg!" Tom yelled, and dove in. I followed.

Instantly the freezing torrent grabbed me and wrenched me
downstream. With the current like a freight train at my backside, I
forced myself up through the murky water towards the yellow light.
At the surface I shouted, and thrashed back to the bridge.

As I clung to the piling, the frothy brown water rushed by. I hung
on for a minute, then had to let go. The torrent swept me to the bank,
where I grabbed a bush, scrambled up the steep dyke and stood
gasping next to Tom.

Dad was still at the car, rummaging for his swim suit. "Goddamit," he shouted, throwing things around in the trunk. "What the hell! It's GODDAM HOT!" He leaned back, tire iron in hand, and wiped sweat off his forehead. "Who the hell stole my suit!" he shouted.

Slamming the trunk, he walked over to the dyke and climbed down to the water. He pulled his threadbare undershirt off over his head, bent down and splashed water on his face and chest. He groaned loudly, then looked over at my brother and shouted, "Where's the towel?"

"There's one on the bridge," Tom replied.

"Christ on a crippled crutch, I wasn't dialing Information. I want the damn thing. Go get it." Tom ran over and brought back the towel — Dad grabbed it from him without a word.

Tom and I swam several races to the big rock in the middle of the canal downstream. Afterwards, we played King of the Mountain for a while, shoving each other off the rock. Finally I crawled up onto the rock to rest, and Tom lay gasping next to me. We lay for a couple of minutes, absorbing the heat of the smooth rock, our feet in the rushing water.

When I got too hot, I stood up and stretched, contemplating the peach orchard beyond the dyke. The trees sagged with fruit, green leaves grey with dust. A picker's ladder was propped against a tree, next to a large wooden bin and stacks of rusty buckets.

Looking back upstream, I could see Dad sitting in the car, tipping a vodka bottle. Just at that moment, Tom shoved me into the stream, shouting "C'mon…bet you can't swim underwater to the other side!" We raced again.

Later I swam upstream and struggled up the timbers to the bridge deck. Dad was at the far end of the bridge, pants half-down, peeing on a cottonwood tree. I hurriedly jumped back into the canal. But when I surfaced, he was standing on the bridge, zipping up his pants, and shouting, "Goddam it, let's go…it's time to go!" He waved at me imperiously.

I swam over to the bank and grabbed the bush, muddy current still ripping at my knees. "But we just got here," I objected.

"Get up here!" he shouted. I started to climb up the bank.

"Just one more race," Tom pleaded.

"NOW! Jump when I say jump, dammit," Dad yelled, scratching his belly.

"We're coming, Dad...." I placated.

"NOW! GODDAMIT!"

Tom, beside me now, stretched to his full height. "You don't have to be so mean about it...."

"Mean? I'll show you mean, you SUPERCILIOUS little sunuv-abitch." Dad stabbed his middle finger at Tom. "You bitch to your mother about mean, I'll show you mean. I've had it up to HERE with your goddam backtalk." Dad strode over to the end of the bridge above us.

"Your problem, you arrogant little SOB, is you've got no respect. NO goddam respect. Come on up here and I'll teach you respect." Dad shook a fist. His face was suddenly crimson, taut white tendons striped his red neck. "You think you're so damn smart, let's see what you can do. Come up here, young buck, and I'll knock that asinine grin off your face...."

Tom shook his head. "I don't want to fight you."

"COME ON! Let's settle this right now, man to man." Dad pointed at the ground in front of him. "I'm still twice the man you are, punk.... GET THE HELL UP HERE! Now!" Suddenly Dad reached down, picked up the vodka bottle and hurled it in our general direction. It shattered on the rocks.

I was shocked. This was more than just the usual yelling.

"Let's beat it," Tom muttered, and dove in. I followed, swimming under the murky water for as long as I could hold my breath, pro-pelled by the current. Finally, I stroked up through the dirty yellow light to the surface. Tom popped up gasping a few feet away.

Behind us, Dad was still shaking his fist. Tom pointed downstream and shouted, "That way!" Panicky, I swam after him. Now Dad would really be mad. Would he drive down the dyke? Drive the car into the ˙canal? Kill us?

Swept along by the current, we swam and drifted, mostly word-less, through the grassy barrens. After two miles, we came to a bridge, climbed out and headed towards home. The blacktop road was too hot for our bare feet, and so was the dirt. So we made our way gingerly, jumping from one clump of roadside weeds to another.

We agreed that if Dad came, we would hide in the ditch. But it never came to that. A farmer gave us a ride home. Dad was in the living room, passed out on the couch.

The thing I remember about Dad is anger. Sometimes he seemed to be pure anger, six feet, 240 pounds, and all of it anger — frightening, overwhelming, dangerous, unpredictable. Actual violence was unusual, but anger was everywhere as he drank himself into an early grave.

If the lead on his pencil broke, he would throw the pencil across the room, with an angry "Jesus Christ on a crooked crutch!" If he couldn't find a tool, if the light bulb burned out, or if he burned a steak on the barbecue, he reacted with a furious expletive.

He never hit me, but his angry bellow commanded my world. In my only recurrent childhood dream, I cowered in outer space before a gigantic Satan. Satan's voice was my dad's bellow.

The Grief He Hid

I never saw Dad's sadness until two years later, just days before he died:

My sister Candy and I were the only ones home. After dinner, Dad approached us and took each of us by the hand — an alien gesture. "Kids, I need to talk to you," he said in an oddly soft voice, looking at us each in turn. "I'm going to die."

I flinched, thinking he might do anything now. Maybe he'd hit me.

Instead, he looked at me and hoarsely whispered, "Will you pray with me?" This was strange. He never implored. And I had never heard him pray — he hadn't attended church since he ran away from home at the age of fourteen. But I looked into his rheumy eyes and nodded.

We followed him into our parents' room. With a sigh he knelt down heavily next to the bed, and Candy and I followed suit. He closed his eyes and I closed mine. As we knelt there, I could smell his sweat, mingled with the floral scent of Mom's night stand powder.

Dad prayed. "Dear Jesus," he said fervently, "I'm a sinner, Lord. I have been mean to my kids, drunk too much, not followed you." He started to cry. I looked over — tears were streaming down his face, his lip was trembling uncontrollably. "I've let down Lucille, let down Franny. I haven't lived a good life, Lord. I've been selfish.... I wish I'd been a better father to my kids.... I'm sorry for letting Candy and Calvin down. I've been a bad father, a terrible father, and I'm sorry Lord...."

I stared for a moment, amazed and frightened, at those trembling lips.

He sniffed hard, clearing his nostrils. "I've sinned, Lord, made so many mistakes, please forgive me.... I've been a rotten husband.... Please Jesus, have mercy on me."

I closed my eyes again. A moment later he put his arm on my shoulder and I could feel his whole body shake. He cried for a long time, making little hiccupy sounds. "I haven't given them what I wanted to give them...." he gasped between hiccups, "I wanted to do a better job for them...."

After a while he got up, and I heard Candy, nine years old, say in a small tense voice, "It's all right, Dad." She gave him a hug. He sniffled and left the room. Afraid to move, I kept my eyes closed and knelt there stiffly for a long time.

Until that night, I had never seen Dad's sadness. Such vulnerability seemed inconceivable. His anger had been omnipresent — but it was only at the threshold of death that he let anyone see his grief.

Instead, like Ahab, Dad smelted his grief into a lifetime of anger. The wounds of his life — his father dying as a missionary in Cuba when Dad was four; a stepfather who favored his natural children over him; his grandfather the minister humiliating him in front of the entire church for teaching other kids how to dance; running away from home at 14; the loneliness and fear of spending his teen years working with a traveling carnival show; the grief of two broken marriages; losing custody of his favorite daughter and never seeing her again; the life wreckage of alcoholism; destruction of a brilliant sales career; the humiliation of losing his job; the shame of being an eighth grade dropout married to a university graduate — all of it boiled down to one, all-consuming emotion.

And his anger left no room for any other feeling.

Anger — The Boy Code's Substitute for Feeling

Today I see a connection between Dad's suppressed grief and his omnipresent anger. I see now that for my dad — and later, for me — anger was a way of avoiding big feelings like grief. Anger is usually a secondary emotion, triggered by an underlying emotion.[2] And men commonly use it to escape their real feelings.

As with many men, Dad's drinking drove his behavior beyond the pale. But Dad simply acted out an exaggerated form of a script that society sanctions. For society actually encourages men to use anger to kill feelings.

As boys, we learn that we should not feel grief, fear, worry, hurt, embarrassment. These are emotions of weakness, vulnerability — sissy stuff. If you show those emotions you will be called a wimp, a pussy, a girlie man. Early on, the Boy Code teaches us to hide such emotions.

However, the Code does allow a man to show one emotion — anger. In patriarchy's crippling split, women are not allowed anger and men are allowed an excess. While it's not OK for men to be vulnerable or sad, anger is a power emotion, so anger is OK. Indeed, it's a high compliment to say of a man "He's a fighter." In traditional patriarchy, it was the *angry* Warrior/King who rose to the top. The patriarch, like Captain Ahab, used anger to cement his position, to demonstrate his power.

Thus, society teaches men to substitute anger for prohibited feelings like sadness and fear. It's a simple thing to do. When one chooses to get angry, adrenaline rushes through the body and triggers the "fight or flight" response. The more primitive parts of the brain engage, and our body surges, preparing to fight. This response makes us feel physically strong, aggressive and in charge. We no longer feel vulnerable. We've driven out the sadness and fear.[3]

So when men face sorrow, we often choose to "cry bullets, not tears." When Ahab loses his leg, he gets angry, not sad. After Dirty Harry's wife dies, Harry gets angry and shoots people.[4] After a woman rejects him, a man doesn't register the real feeling of hurt. Instead, he swiftly moves to angry blame ("the bitch"). After a child scares him by running into the street, a man forgets the scare and yells angrily at the kid. After the boss criticizes him, a man doesn't process the sadness — he just blows up later at somebody else.

We escape from feelings into anger. We close our hearts and put up our dukes. In this way, we maintain both our power and the Male Mask — but we forfeit our real feelings. We pay a price for this.

The Cost of Chronic Anger

The cost of chronic anger is high. Two days after the night he cried, anger killed my dad. At the age of 50, he was struck by a fatal chest hemorrhage as he tried to rage a stalled car back to life. He joined the millions of angry men that have raged themselves to death.

Anger is fatal for men like Dad. The ancient prophet warned that "Wrath kills the foolish man," and modern science confirms it. Chronically angry men are three times more likely to have a heart attack than low anger men and are at higher risk for stroke. Studies have shown that angry men are more likely to be involved in serious accidents. No wonder that Buddha identified anger as the first of the Three Poisons.[5]

Anger not only damages health. It also cuts a destructive swathe through our relationships, killing many, crippling others. Dad's anger alienated him from his wife and children — he died a lonely death, having seriously hurt the family he loved.

And anger begets violence. Anger can lead to insults, violent outbursts and assaults. At its extreme, it can lead to murder, suicide, terrorism and war. Much of the world's violence — between both spouses and nations — could be avoided, if men didn't deny their vulnerable feelings and transform them into anger.

═══ Constructive Anger (Respectful Assertiveness) ═══

Of course, there are times when anger is appropriate. When someone crosses my boundaries or violates my rights, it's healthy to clarify my boundaries right away, set limits and ask them to change their behavior. Constructive anger expresses what I want and need, without putting the other person down. It protests, but does not *blame*. It asserts, "I felt bad when you did that. I want you to act differently." — Not, "You are a jerk for doing that."

Constructive anger is respectful, and values both me and the other person. It asserts my independence, but invites positive negotiation in the relationship.[6]

On the other hand, chronic anger is a serious problem. Such anger is more than a response to a particular provocation. It's a general attitude towards life — an attitude that routinely invokes anger to replace other feelings. This habitual anger disrespects others, and lacks a sense of proportion. By its nature it is aimed at blame, not solutions. It doesn't change bad situations, it just endlessly decries them.[7]

Chronic anger keeps a man from noticing his true feelings, and accepting himself as he actually is. It keeps him from taking care of himself. Most tragically, habitual anger destroys his relationship with himself.[8]

The Path to Chronic Anger — How the Anger Habit Works

Despite the costs, many men have the anger habit. They routinely choose thoughts that lead to anger.

The first thing to understand is that, to a large extent, the *thoughts* we choose determine our feelings. Exactly the same thing can happen to three different people, and one will react with anger, one with sadness, and one with equanimity. The difference is how they think about it.

For example, if a car crashes through the front door of a restaurant, one patron may react with outrage to the event. Another will sit and sip his coffee and watch events unfold. Yet another may become shaken and anxious, as a result of the same intrusion. The event is exactly the same — the difference is how each of them thinks about it. As Epictetus noted, "Men are not troubled by things themselves, but by their thoughts about them."[9]

According to cognitive behavior theory, if I choose to think about a life event with:

- Thoughts of danger — I will feel *anxiety/fear*.
- Thoughts that diminish me (thoughts of failure and rejection) — I will feel s*ad*.
- Thoughts of gain and self-enhancement — I will feel *pleasure*.
- Thoughts that someone has wronged (attacked) me — I will feel *anger*.[10]

As we've learned, the Boy Code does not allow men to experience sadness and fear. From boyhood we have learned it is shameful for males to cry or be afraid — it is more acceptable to feel angry. So when we begin to feel sadness or fear, many men have learned to steer our thoughts down the path to anger.

The mental sequence that frequently takes us down the Anger Path is:

| Event | → | Interpreting it negatively (as failure, rejection, self-diminishment, dangerous, etc) | → | Feeling distressed (sad, fearful, etc) | → | Thoughts of being wronged | → | Anger (shifts focus to others) |

Adapted from Beck, *Prisoners of Hate*, p. 31.

How do I get from feeling distressed to anger? The key step is transforming the distress into the anger-provoking thought: *I have been wronged (i.e., attacked)*. It works like this:

1. I'm distressed (sad, fearful, etc.).
2. I think this feeling is unmanly and wrong.
3. Since I cannot accept this prohibited feeling, I conclude
   a. I *should* not feel distressed.
   b. Therefore, you *should* not have done whatever it was that triggered my distress.
4. Thus, you have *wronged* (attacked) me. You have made me feel emotions a man must not feel.
5. I must fight to defend myself from being wronged. Now I am angry.

As I get angry, my thoughts and bodily responses escalate each other. Angry thoughts ("I've been attacked") trigger adrenaline production — the body's "fight or flight" response to attack. The brain senses the adrenaline rush and thinks, "This must be a crisis!" The brain reacts by creating more angry exaggerated thoughts. In turn, these thoughts prompt the production of more adrenaline, which triggers more exaggerated thoughts, which triggers more adrenaline. Soon I feel powerful. The sadness is forgotten — all I feel is anger.[11]

Many men habitually travel this Anger Path. In fact they've traveled it so often it's almost hardwired in their nervous system.[12] When they feel distressed, they automatically think that someone must have *wronged* them. They never even notice the underlying distress, just the reactive anger.

Of course, the fundamental problem with the Anger Path is that it rejects reality. It rejects the truth that I am now feeling vulnerable — and insists that things *should* be different. Instead of accepting what I am actually feeling, I blame you for making me feel unacceptable emotions.

I blame you, instead of experiencing me.

My Journey Down the Anger Path

The sins of the fathers [are visited] upon the children,
and upon the children's children,
unto the third and to the fourth generation.

Exodus 34:7

Until recently, my conversations with myself often led me down the Anger Path. I spoke to myself as a Harsh Father — as my father had spoken to me, and as his grandfather had spoken to him. I was often critical and cruel to myself — which made me feel sad, afraid, anxious, helpless, hurt, worried or embarrassed. Feeling bad, I would then "talk myself up" into anger at someone, in order to get rid of vulnerable feelings. I would find somebody to blame, so I could replace my vulnerable feelings with powerful anger.

Cognitive behaviour researchers like Dr. Aaron Beck have documented how such self-dialogue transforms feelings of vulnerability into anger.[13] My own dialogues worked this way:

- If I was trying to fix a faucet, and I couldn't get it to work, I would often feel *frustrated and helpless*. Then I would tell myself, *"God, you're incompetent."* Reacting to my Harsh Father's criticism, I would feel vulnerable — but only for a second. I would quickly divert the blame onto the hardware clerk. The next thing I'd be swearing, "That bloody clerk! This goddam thing… I think they sold me the wrong part." Now I felt angry instead of *helpless*.
- If I was at the office on the weekend preparing a docu-

ment, and I couldn't get the computer to work, I'd feel *anxious*. I'd say to myself, *"Damn, you're not going to be able to figure this out. You're so bad with computers."* With heightened anxiety, I'd quickly reflect that blame away from me. *"Nobody's here to help, and that's typical. They all go home right at 4:30 on Friday, and leave me to fend for myself. And I don't even get credit for it — in fact, if I'm a bit late on Monday morning, they'll begrudge me that!"* By this time I'd be so worked up that it would be difficult to figure out the computer problem — but I felt powerfully angry, instead of *anxious*.

- Trying to buy shoes on sale, I felt *embarrassed* if the clerk refused the sale price and pointed out that I'd missed the small print in the ad that limited the sale offer. I would harshly say to myself: *"Now, how did I miss that, knucklehead?"* But I didn't simply acknowledge I'd made a mistake, register my embarrassment, reassure myself and move on with my life.

  Instead, I would channel that embarrassment into anger — first into anger at myself ("knucklehead"), and then into anger at the clerk. I'd say, *"That's just crooked, how small that print is. That's just made to mislead."* In my head, I'd "build a case" about how deceitful the store was. I'd get sarcastic to the clerk, perhaps raise my voice, get blaming. Soon I no longer felt *sad* about myself.

- If we were late for a social engagement and my wife and kids were dawdling, I'd feel *frustrated and afraid* that we were going to be late. I'd say to myself harshly, *"People are going to think I'm rude and inconsiderate."* But instead of registering my fear and embarrassment, accepting the situation and moving on to a solution (like the simple one of phoning ahead, apologizing for being late, and letting them know I was trying to get there), I'd blame my wife. I'd say to myself, *"She's always late. She thinks I'm unimportant. She's so inconsiderate!"* To the family, I'd snap,

"For Christ's sake, let's go!" The payoff was that now I was feeling angry instead of *afraid and embarrassed.*
- If my wife felt sad, I would feel *sad*. But I couldn't acknowledge my sadness. Instead, I would follow the familiar "anger path" of thought — blaming myself and then her. First I would think, *"It's my fault. I should be able to cheer her up, but I'm not a good enough husband."* That would heighten my sadness and shame, which I had to get rid of by blaming her. Soon I would be angry, chiding her to "get on with it" and stop "wallowing" in her feelings. Unable to deal with my feelings, I used anger to control hers instead.

The pattern was consistent. An event would happen that I interpreted negatively. I would feel a painful feeling for a fleeting moment. My Harsh Father (internal critic) would automatically blame me. This would create or exacerbate a rush of negative feeling — and I would try to get rid of that feeling by blaming and getting angry at others.

Even when my painful feelings came from pure acts of fate — not from negative self-talk — I reacted in the same way. If I almost fell off a ladder and scared myself, I'd look around for somebody to blame. If a friend was diagnosed with cancer, I wouldn't cry. But hours later I'd be snapping at somebody.

In sum, I was in the "Anger Habit." I used anger like a drug, to keep painful feelings at bay. Repetition of blaming thoughts reinforced the neurological pathway for anger in my brain — and banished vulnerable feelings from my heart.[14]

Farewell to the Anger Habit — Feeling My Own Feelings

*Mental health is an ongoing process
of dedication to reality at all costs.*[15]

The opposite of the Anger Habit dynamic is to accept what is — to accept my feelings and process them. It involves fully experiencing my feelings, instead of rejecting them and converting them into anger.[16] It requires me to drop the Masculine Mask, and allow my Authentic Self to feel his life.

Often it's enough to just honestly and calmly acknowledge to myself that I'm feeling something painful. Sometimes that leads to deeper feelings. Either way, I avoid turning the pain into counterfeit anger.

The surprise is how wonderful it is to honestly confront the feelings I spent a lifetime avoiding. After decades of never crying, I've discovered that even big feelings won't kill me. I have found that fully experiencing an emotion is actually grounding and satisfying. It's not difficult or complex — it's way easier than suppressing emotion or masking it with anger.

In fact, I have learned that I can pass through an emotion, cry healing tears, and move on, actually liberated and enriched by the experience. When my daughter was eight, I learned this valuable lesson from her. At a very difficult time in her life, she became terribly sad, threw herself on the bed and cried her heart out. I was frightened by the intensity of her grief and her heart-rending tears, and was tempted to shut her down by cosseting or coercing. But fortunately I just listened, and she cried it out. To my amazement, minutes later she bounced up, smiling and then laughing. She had passed through the feeling and on to the other side.

She intuitively knew the wisdom that Buddhism teaches:

When unpleasant feelings arise, and we try to avoid them, we set up a chain reaction of entanglement and suffering. This perpetuates the body of fear. However, if we learn to be aware of feelings without grasping or aversion, then they can move through us like changing weather, and we can be free to feel them and move on like the wind.[17]

Contrary to the belief of many men, our feelings will not kill us. We don't have to escape to anger. We can feel and process our vulnerable feelings — and let them move through us like changing weather. And, like my daughter, we can bounce back smiling and laughing.

> *The deeper that sorrow carves into your being, the more joy you can contain.*[18]

How this approach works

As I have discussed in previous chapters, if I have established a relationship with myself by

- holding myself in friendly regard — acting as a Kind Father and Best Friend to myself,
- paying attention to my feelings,
- identifying and articulating the feelings to myself and others,
- giving myself permission to feel the feelings and grieve them, if necessary,
- sharing the feelings and listening to others' feelings,

I will be able to experience feelings of distress, and pass through them. I do not have to be ashamed of those feelings, and obliterate them with angry blame.

Nowadays when I am hurt by something, I don't just immediately divert myself with work or activity the way I used to. When I first feel a distressing emotion, I take the time to *pay attention* to it, feel it and process it. I give myself the time, right then, to pay attention to what I'm feeling, feel it, phone up a friend and process it. This helps avoid the phenomenon of submerging the feeling — only to have it emerge later as anger.

Paying attention has another advantage. If someone is doing something annoying, I will see it — and express my concern early on, in a reasonable way. I can respectfully ask them to stop, and hopefully they will. That way I don't wait until they've repeatedly crossed my boundaries — and react with stored-up anger.

But it's my relationship with the Kind Father that is most important in avoiding the Anger Path. The fact is, the kinder I am to myself, the kinder I will be to others. If I talk to myself in the way that nurturing people have spoken to me in the past, I'm less likely to become angry. This self-talk gives me encouragement, support, a sense of gain and self-enhancement — thoughts that lead to pleasure, instead of distress and anger.[19]

On the other hand, if my self-talk is blaming — if the Harsh Father speaks — I head down the Anger Path. If I am critical and blaming with myself, I will eventually be the same to others. The fundamental principle is that the way I treat myself is eventually reflected in the way I treat others.

Thus, I must stop being cruel to myself if I want to curb my anger. As Thich Nhat Hanh the noble teacher from Vietnam has written, stopping anger begins with the following principle: "No enemies. Begin with yourself."[20]

Now in stressful situations, I try to be kind to myself. I ask myself: *What would a Kind Father say to me in this situation?* And then I visualize the Kind Father helping me deal with my feelings. Instead of abusing myself, talking myself up to anger and fleeing from the root emotion, the Kind Father helps me to acknowledge my root feeling. Then he goes on to reassure, support and encourage me:

> *You'll be OK. Relax, and take care of yourself. What are you feeling here? I know you feel frustrated. I feel for you, buddy. This is a really frustrating, tough situation. I appreciate how you're doing. I want to encourage you to deal with this calmly.*

He reminds me that I can speak as a constant friend to myself, not a foe. He repeatedly gives me kind messages:

> *I respect you.*
> *I encourage you.*

I support you.
I admire particular things that you do.
I like particular things about you.

For example, in the situation described earlier where my computer broke on the weekend, I might imagine the Kind Father saying this to me:

Take a few minutes to walk around the block and take care of yourself. Take a deep breath. Have a glass of juice. Now, be nice to yourself. I appreciate how hard you're working. I respect the way you're taking care of yourself and respecting others.

It's only natural for you to feel uptight because of the deadline. But you've dealt with these before. You'll figure out a solution to this — you always have in the past.

I know it's frustrating to be here alone with this problem, but I really like the fact you are so dedicated to your work. I admire that perseverance.

I want to encourage you to be gentle with yourself. Even if the worst were to happen and the project was a bit late, or a bit imperfect, I want to encourage you to be kind to yourself. You are a worthy human being for so many reasons, a good father and friend. No outcome of this project can undermine that.

We can come up with a strategy for dealing with deadlines later, arrange for support staff to come in and help in these situations, so we can avoid this difficulty in the future. I really respect the kind way you are dealing with a difficult situation.

When I was frustrated fixing the faucet, the Kind Father might say:

Boy, you're really feeling frustrated. I know you want to get this fixed, and fixing faucets always makes you anxious — it makes you feel like you're not a real man, because this stuff is challenging for you.... But you're good at your work. You don't have to be perfect at plumbing too. I respect you for giving it a try. A lot of people just call the plumber. I respect your dedication to getting this done, and you always get it done, even if it ain't pretty.

I know you're feeling frustrated. It's normal to feel frustration sometimes — anyone would be when the faucet breaks like that. Problems are a normal part of life. I guess this is going to be one of those hard days.

You'll deal with it, and I respect the fact you're doing it without anger. You're having a Big Feeling, but this is not a catastrophic life event — you're just feeling the effects of adrenaline.

I encourage you to go ask Robin for help. That will be less frustrating, because he's done this type of faucet before. You don't have to do it all, control it all. Relax and see how this works out. Maybe Robin and you will have a good chat while you figure it out. This actually could be an opportunity to get to know him.

I respect the calm way you're dealing with this, and respecting people.

As the Kind Father encourages me, I develop a different, gentler approach. For example, when denied the sale price for shoes, I might respond to the Kind Father like this:

OK, I guess I missed the small print. Well, I guess I'll just have to accept that that price isn't available. I'll take a look around and see if there's something else here that might be good. Or I can go down the street and look. Maybe it wasn't meant to be — maybe I'll get a better deal elsewhere.

Darn, now there's a long lineup. Oh, well, these clerks are really busy. They look overworked. I will smile at the

clerk, and look at the newspaper while I'm waiting.... I
can't make this lineup move any faster with will power, so I
think I'll just accept it and enjoy the experience of being in
line. I wonder what this rose smells like? M-m-m-m, that's
nice.... Maybe a friend will come along and we'll have a
great chat. Maybe God's agenda will be more rewarding
than mine.

Since I'm already downtown, I think I'll make the best
of it — there's a good movie on, or I could phone Mary and
have a chat.

And the Kind Father replies:

I really like how calmly you're dealing with this. You're re-
ally getting it — life is a journey, not a destination.

Those raised by healthy parents effortlessly engage in these
kind of reassuring inner dialogues all the time. By osmosis,
they have integrated the parental encouragement and support
they received as children. But for the average man, it's not so
easy. He needs to first discover the Kind Father — and then
learn how to act as a Kind Father to himself.

The bonus is that by doing so, he inevitably becomes a
kinder father to his own kids. He not only takes care of himself — he begins to break the Chain of Anger that spans generations.

Alternatives to the Anger Path

I have learned other effective ways to avoid anger:
- I take a "time out" when I get into a heated situation.
  When my pulse rises to 100, I need to leave the conversation. At that point science tells us that a person is cogni-
  tively impaired — I can't rationally hear what the other
  person is saying. The more primitive parts of the brain are
  kicking in, and I'm more likely to get angry and say something regrettable.[21]

Instead, I go for a walk, talk kindly to myself or distract myself for a while. It often helps to call a friend and ask for emotional support. After an hour, if my pulse has been normal for a while, I can rejoin the other person.

- I am careful to not "build a case" against the other person. I used to justify myself by cataloguing all the other person's misdeeds and faults. This gave me a justification for being angry, and heightened the emotion.

  Now if I see that I'm talking myself into blaming the other person, I just say to myself, as a Kind Father would say to a son, "I encourage you to stop talking yourself up. This is not a road you want to go down — it won't accomplish anything good. You don't want to experience the negative impacts of anger, so don't go there."[22]

- When I talk to myself about a tough situation, I am careful not to use *inflammatory words*. I say, "This is challenging" or "frustrating" — but I avoid using swear words or catastrophizing words like, "This is a disaster," or "a fucking failure." And I avoid absolute words like "She *never...*He *always.*" Anthony Robbins discusses how using aggressive metaphors like "He's holding a gun to my head," "Life is war," and "Dog eat dog" creates emotions that are unnecessarily heated. For example, Robbins found that simply changing his description of interchanges with his wife from "intense arguments" to "spirited debates" lowered the temperature in his marriage.[23]

- When angry or frustrated I used to ceaselessly worry at the problem — and spend a lot of time trying to convince the other person that I was right. That often just led to new flare-ups. I'm now cautious about trying to justify myself when I'm still upset. Often it's better for me to contact a friend instead, and talk out my feelings with someone less reactive.

- Often I get angry because somebody is not doing what I want them to do. As an alternative to trying to control

their behavior (a sure recipe for frustration and anger), I
simply do what I wanted done myself.

- I try to not condemn myself. Men often bitterly condemn
themselves as jerks for the last time they got angry. Paradoxically, if a man condemns himself, he's more likely to
turn around and get angry again later. The fact is, blame is
indivisible — if I blame myself, I will eventually get back
to blaming you.

  So, if I've made a mistake, I try to acknowledge it
— and then warmly encourage myself to take a different
course of action. But I don't condemn myself. Encouragement improves behavior, while condemnation is counter-
productive.

- When I handle a tough situation without getting angry, I
give myself a pat on the back: "Hey, nice going, that was a
tough situation, and you played it cool..." I reward myself for managing my emotions well. Positive reinforce-
ment works.

As I have put the above into practice, I have discovered that I
am no longer "hardwired" for anger. Over time I have actually perceived a change in my physiological response to stressful situations. Now I don't easily feel the "rush of anger." I
am not wearing out my body — and my relationships — with
unnecessary anger.

Conclusion

I am my father's rage,
and if I don't heal that rage,
my sons will be their father's rage.[24]

Captain Ahab lies in wreckage at the bottom of the ocean, near Moby
Dick. The rope around the Captain's neck flutters in the deep currents,
still anchored to the harpoon in the whale's side.

Dad lies alone in a graveyard, just a few miles from the canal where he terrorized us.

If Dad had only known how to avoid the Anger Path, he might still be with us today. He might have met his grandchildren. He and I might not have lost the love we once had for each other. He might not have plunged into the long dark night alone.

He might have learned to become his own best friend — and mine. He might have shared the hard things in his life with me — and the joys. Today I'd like to ask him what it was like when he fell in love with Mom, and how he felt the day I was born. I'd like to hear what it was like for him the day he lost his job — and compare notes with him about turning 50. I'd like to know what he thought about the meaning of life, and what his trick was for making great Mulligan stew. But our conversations at his grave are one-sided.

Men like Dad and me have good reasons to abandon chronic anger. Habitual anger makes us ill, hurts us emotionally, fails to get us what we ultimately want, and isolates us from family, friends and others. It cuts us off from our real feelings — we become strangers to ourselves.

The good news is that we can break the Anger Habit.

Instead of living the life that the Boy Code tells us we "should," we can live a real life of our own. We can feel our real feelings and be our real selves. Instead of angrily blaming others when we experience prohibited feelings, we can take care of ourselves. We can experience the pleasure that comes from moving through our real feelings — and the serenity that comes with learning how to manage them. We can learn to be our own Kind Fathers, our own best friends.

I wish Dad had known this.

Forgiveness and Freedom

To forgive is to set a prisoner free
and discover that the prisoner was you.

— Lewis Smedes

My dad held everyone to the strictest standards. He never forgave himself, and seldom forgave others. He died blaming everybody:

On the day Dad died, he was driving us to school in our ten-year-old Plymouth. Halfway there, the engine died, and the car glided down a suddenly silent dirt road. "Oh, for CHRIST'S sake!" Dad exclaimed, and pulled over onto the shoulder. He hit the brakes hard — almost throwing me into the steel dash.

Behind me, my sister Pam rebounded off the seat-back, clutching her second-grade reader to her chest. Next to her, nine-year-old Candy spilled her lunch bucket with a clatter. Pam fell back into the rear seat, exhaling heavily, "Whoo!"

Dad tried to start the car. Click. "Goddamit!" he muttered, repeatedly turning the key on and off. Nothing. He tried again, then sat back and glared at the silent ignition, "Don't do this to me, you rusty sunuvabitch!"

One more try. No luck. "Jesus Christ on a crippled crutch!" he muttered, as he jerked the hood release. He struggled to raise his heavy body out of the driver's seat and step outside, slamming the door behind him.

As the girls whispered tensely in the back seat, I sat in the front and watched Dad. For a moment he just stood there, frowning at the cattle in the field, squinting into the brilliant spring morning. The green grasslands, carpeted with tiny red and yellow flowers, stretched across a small prairie to Submarine Hill. Scores of tiny cotton puffs drifted down from the tall cottonwoods along the nearby stream and filled the air around Dad. Sweat beading on his forehead in the warm early light, Dad swatted the fluff out of his face. He took a soft pack of Camels out of his pocket, lit one and took a deep drag, sourly contemplating failure.

"That bastard Armstrong," he finally muttered, throwing the fresh cigarette down and grinding it under his shoe. "Whatta piece of junk!" Shaking his head, he lumbered over to the trunk and rummaged around, returning with a screwdriver. Fury building, he heaved the hood open. "Goddam that Armstrong to hell, anyway!"

From where I sat, I could look through the hood opening and see Dad's hands working aimlessly in the engine compartment, the anchor tattoo on his forearm moving in and out of view. He lifted the battery off its platform, and probed below with the screwdriver. A minute later he jerked back, shaking a nicked finger. "Sweet Jesus!"

But he didn't stop to take care of it. Instead, he leaned back into the engine — and railed against the man who sold him the car last year. "I never should have trusted that sunuvabitch Armstrong! I never should have believed him.... He screwed me! 'Sound as a dollar', my ass!"

Candy and Pam huddled in the far corner of the back seat, whispering. They giggled once. I checked the car clock. "I don't want to be late for school, Dad," I called out. "Should we go ahead and walk?" He pulled back from the hood and stared at me through the windshield — blankly, as if I were a stranger. After a moment, he looked away, "What the hell do I care?" Bending back under the hood, he mumbled something. I didn't move.

Finally Dad got back in, seat springs groaning under his weight. He wiped his bloody finger on the engine rag, then threw the rag onto the floor in front of me. "Now this had better work!" He turned the key back and forth several times. At one point the engine started to catch. "Oh, baby," Dad coaxed hopefully, "Oh, baby…come on." The engine shuddered for a full minute, rattled, then died.

Dad leaned back, and sighed heavily. He turned and looked out the window — the cotton puffs drifted across the sky, a legion of tiny parachutes. Finally he sat up and smacked the steering wheel as hard as he could. I jerked involuntarily.

"JEEZ-US, just shoot me if I ever deal with that crook again…. Nothing but sunuvabitchin' headaches. THE GODDAM CON!"

At this point, I turned, gave the girls a meaningful look and discretely gathered up my books. "OK, Dad, we'd better go," I ventured quietly. He didn't respond, so we got out and started to walk away. "Bye, Dad," Candy called out to him.

"Yeah, yeah," he growled, shaking his head, impatiently waving us away.

"C'mon," I urged, "we can't be late." Pam took my hand.

As we walked down the road, I could hear him in the distance: "That bastard Armstrong had the nerve! Palming this off on me!" he shouted. I looked back in time to see him raise his right fist and slam it down onto the steel fender. "Goddam HIM to HELL!" The fender reverberated, a heavy hollow sound.

The car never did start — it had to be towed. And I never spoke to Dad again. He died late that night, as the arteries in his chest burst from ancient blame.

In his last years, this was my Father. Consumed by failure, first he blamed himself — then he blamed others. It was all some son-of-a-bitch's fault. He forgave no one. Tom Armstrong was just the latest in a long line of people that he blamed his life on.

And in the end, this man who routinely inflicted blame on others was the one who suffered the most. Refusing to give himself and others a simple break, he alienated family and friends. He missed his last chance to say goodbye to his kids. He died in an empty hospital room.

It's a paradox. Dad's refusal to forgive others destroyed him.

The Country of Resentment

Resentment is like taking poison
and waiting for the other person to die.
— Malachy McCourt

In the years since Dad died, I've seen many others destroyed by blame. As a young social worker on Vancouver's skid row, I met scores of men who were consumed by their own bitterness — by their resentment of family members, former wives, lovers and friends.

They nursed their bitterness, and it was killing them. They drank, drugged or angered themselves to death. It's a fool's game.

Sam was about 60, an alcoholic and fitness fanatic. He kept a set of weights in his derelict hotel room, and spent hours alternating between lifting them, and inspecting his body in a cracked full-length mirror. He'd stand in the middle of the room in his worn blue gym shorts and stained t-shirt, lift the barbell and then slowly bring it down. "Damn, I'm in better shape now than when I was twenty!" he'd exclaim, pointing proudly at the mirror and flexing his bicep.

With no fridge in his room, he kept his cheap white wine chilled on the bird crap-encrusted ledge outside his window. And he kept his bitterness fresh — and served daily — against the woman who had wronged him. He told the story of how she ruined his life to everyone that came along. "We had the finest house in the Valley, and I drove a brand new Cadillac. Every two years a spanking new Seville. I gave her everything I had, and she left me with nothing, the bitch! She got the mine, I got the shaft.... Plus, she ruined my health! I've never been the same."

He finished the story, lifted up the barbell and did a chest press — then took a swig of his ever-present wine bottle. "Goddamned women." Putting down his bottle, he looked straight at me with his milky blue eyes, wrinkled face pursing around the incongruous perfection of false teeth. "You're a young man," he muttered. "Let me give you one piece of advice, and I won't even charge."

"OK."

With slow deliberation, he propped one foot on the barbell, wiped a splotchy arm across his face, and stared at me for a long time. Finally, he shook his head, shrugging off last night's hangover. "Don't trust a woman," he whispered. "They'll ruin you."

Then he would drink the alcohol that was killing him.

The bitterness ate him up — dominated his days, and his conversations with strangers like me. Ironically, it had no effect whatsoever on the woman. She was unaware, never saw him — had established her own separate life in a distant town years ago.

Dad and Sam are extreme examples, but millions live as if life's central purpose was to answer an Existential question — "Who is to *Blame*?" If something goes wrong in their lives, somebody has to be to blame. When finances, relationships or cars break down, they escape their feelings of disappointment by blaming somebody. They don't forgive mistakes — theirs or yours.

Such people live their lives in what psychologist Robert Karen has called the "Country of Resentment".[1] This Country has rigid rules about what people *should do* and *should not do*. In this Resentful Land:

- My dad *should* have been successful, so he'd have a newer car;
- Tom Armstrong *should* have sold him a car that would never break; and
- Sam's lover *should* have stayed with him.

Life becomes a tyranny of *shoulds*. Instead of accepting what is, the Citizens of Resentment blame each other for not doing, being or feeling something else. In life's greatest folly, they refuse to accept reality — instead they insist on what *should* have been.

I settled early in the Country of Resentment. Because I didn't drink, my Blame Game was not as blatant as Dad's or Sam's. But the basic approach was similar — I blamed myself and others for what we *should* have done.

I did it with little things. When I was in a rush and the office stapler was empty, I'd quietly fume about how staff *should* have filled it. If my takeout coffee spilled when I added cream, I'd deal with my embarrassment by blaming the waiter under my breath for overfilling the cup. Instead of just shrugging and cleaning up life's inevitable mishap, I'd fume to myself about what the waiter *should* have done.

If I was entertaining guests and wanted them to have a perfect visit, I had a fixed idea of how things *should* be. And if things fell short — if the dinner I cooked wasn't ideal, or the theater we went to wasn't open — I would lay blame. I blamed myself, and blamed others. I compared everything with what I'd planned — and found reality wanting.

And I was equally unforgiving about big things. For example, I spent a lifetime blaming my dad for not being the dad he *should* have been.

Whether the event was big or small, I didn't accept what was, and move on. Instead, I thought of what *should* have been — and looked for somebody to blame. This came at great cost to me and others.

Failing to Forgive — The Costs

My blaming lifestyle clearly made the people around me miserable. But it also damaged my body and crippled me emotionally. In *Forgive for Good*, Stanford University's Fred Luskin has detailed the physiology of how we damage ourselves when we fail to forgive.

Typically, we start off by developing a "grievance story" about the wrong. Major grievance stories include things like:

- *My dad beat me and injured me beyond repair.*
- *My mother always put me down and I've never been able to hold my head up since.*
- *My wife left me and heartlessly destroyed my life.*
- *My life would have been all right if that bastard drunk driver hadn't killed my brother in 1978.*
- *My boss laid me off and threw my career into a tailspin.*

Later, when we feel bad for whatever reason, instead of fully processing the new feeling, we tell ourselves the grievance story from the past.

Some stories (e.g., about spilled coffee or a driver cutting us off) may be repeated for just a short period. But major stories can be repeated hundreds of times over the years — both to ourselves and to other people. Sam endlessly repeated the story of the woman who wronged him; Dad of the people who'd cheated him. I told myself the story of how Dad abused me.

The wrongdoer may be dead, twenty years long gone, or in Southeast Asia. In some cases the person may not have thought of me in years. But they remain a powerful figure in my mind, as I reenact the scene repeatedly in a fruitless attempt to change the past.

The problem is that each time the story is rehearsed, *the negative event is experienced again.* As the grudge is rehearsed mentally, it triggers a physiological response similar to the one experienced during the actual event. My mind's reenactment of the original trauma causes my body to produce stress hormones, which raise my blood pressure and heartbeat. I begin to feel angry and helpless all over again — about an event that happened years ago.[2]

With a single grievance, I can trigger the "fight or flight" response in myself hundreds of times, as I tell the same story over and over. And each time I cause myself pain and physical stress.

Stanford University's Forgiveness Project has documented how habitual rehearsal of grievance stories damages health. Habitual blame is linked to depression, a lack of optimism and a loss in self-confidence. People who blame others for their problems have higher rates of cardiovascular disease and cancer and suffer more from a variety of illnesses.[3]

In Dad's case, his blaming habit killed him.

Continuing to blame disempowers me

Constant repetition of a grievance story also robs me of personal power. For example, Sam's habit of blaming stripped him of authentic power — he gave it away to the woman who had "wronged" him. He'd convinced himself that she had all the power — and he was just a victim.

The fact is, when I repeatedly tell myself that I am the victim of a wrongdoer, I encourage a dangerous belief — that I can't be fixed unless the wrongdoer changes. I continue to give up my power to someone I have no control over, to a person who has previously hurt me. I convince myself that I have no power except the power to blame.

Desmond Tutu tells the story of the bitter former prisoner of war who gathered with other POWs at the Vietnam Memorial in Washington, DC. His comrade asked him:

> *"Have you forgiven those who held you prisoner of war?"*
> *"I will never forgive them,"* he replied.

His friend stared at him:

> *"Then it seems they still have you in prison, don't they?"*[4]

To reclaim authentic power, I must stop re-enacting my victimization and move on. By choosing to forgive, I stop picturing myself as victim — and again cast myself as the hero in my life's odyssey. I begin to focus again on what I can do, not what has been done to me. I regain the power to make my own life.

Continuing to blame blocks feelings and prevents healing and growth

One of the most tragic things about my unforgiving lifestyle was that it kept me from having an authentic relationship with myself. Focusing blame on other people diverted me from my own feelings. My grievance stories about them distracted me from what I was actually feeling. As long as I focused on Dad's flaws, I couldn't feel my own pain.

Thus, I never had a chance to really mourn and move on to healing. When I blamed others, I stopped the healing process of experiencing, processing and moving through my own feelings. As psychologist Robert Karen says, "Blame is the anti-mourn and, hence, the anti-self... the more we blame, the further we get from ourselves."[5]

Karen has noted a striking pattern. His patients who fail to forgive do not heal. In contrast, those who learn to forgive go on to heal and grow. The relationship between forgiveness and mental health is clear. In one survey, ninety-three per cent of mental health professionals agreed that forgiving one's parents or others is a prerequisite for mental health.[6]

Tragically, Dad never forgave — and went to his grave with old wounds that he had never tended.

Continuing to Blame Destroys Lives

Finally, the failure to forgive is source of a large portion of human misery. The failure to forgive small things taints day-to-day social interactions. And the failure to forgive big things ruins relationships and families, and fills lives with bitterness. For example, many people go to a lonely grave, simply because they cannot find their way to forgive a brother, a sister, a parent. Arguably, the failure to forgive has caused everything from World War II to a million divorces a year.

In a sense, we all live out the tragedy of *Romeo and Juliet.* Just as the grudge between the Montagues and Capulets destroyed the most exquisite love the world has ever known, so do our resentments threaten the love and joy in our lives.

We can learn from this. Shakespeare's feuding families only learned to forgive after finding their beloved children dead, embracing in the tomb — the poison at Romeo's side, the dagger in Juliet's breast. The Prince points to the lovers and chides their fathers for not forgiving each other:

> Capulet! Montague!
> See what a scourge is laid upon your hate,
> That heav'n finds means to kill your joys with love! [7]

At that point, Romeo's father repents — he vows to melt down his fortune into a gold statue of his foe's dead daughter. Juliet's father vows to make a similar monument to Romeo. But in the end they are two old men, left with nothing but metal statues of dead children.

Shakespeare had it right. In ways both big and small, the failure to forgive kills love and murders beauty. An unforgiving attitude makes life far less loving and beautiful than it could be.

Moving from Blame to Forgiveness

I spent years living in the Country of Resentment. But, today I find it much more satisfying to experience my feelings than to blame them on somebody else. I have discovered I can move through my feelings — even bad ones — to real connection with myself and others.

And, because I have learned to
- become a good friend and a Kind Father to myself;
- give myself encouragement and support, instead of habitual criticism;
- pay attention to my feelings and identify what it is that I'm feeling;
- experience my feelings fully, mourning fully;

- share my heart experience with others and experience the connection of listening to their experiences,

I have become more forgiving. I don't have to get angry and blame others to escape my feelings — because now I welcome my feelings. In short, establishing a relationship with myself has helped free me from the blaming lifestyle.

Another factor has helped. In the difficult time I have passed through in recent years, I have regularly concluded

─────────────── **What is forgiveness?** ───────────────

The dictionary defines forgiveness: "To stop feeling angry or resentful towards someone for an offence, flaw or mistake."[8]

Experts tell us that forgiveness is:

- Letting go of a negative attachment to the past.
- Letting go of the intense emotions tied to the past event — recognizing I no longer need to hold onto grudges, resentments, hatred and self pity.
- Recognizing people are different, want and need different things and sometimes hurt each other.
- No longer blaming the other person for my feelings.
- No longer wanting to punish, realizing that punishing another will not heal me.
- Moving on. Freeing my energy, and putting it to better use.[9]

But forgiveness is not:

- Excusing or condoning the wrong. I can hold the person accountable before forgiving. Confrontation and truthtelling may be necessary first.
- Necessarily reconciliation. If the person is bad for me, I need not have anything further to do with them.
- Tolerating bad actions. Forgiveness doesn't require me to get hurt again, or allow a recurrence.
- Giving up a claim to justice. Forgiveness doesn't deny that a wrong took place.
- Forgetting. I don't erase the wrong from my mind — I just don't let it dominate my life.
- Denying my pain. In fact forgiveness allows me to reconnect with my feelings, once I move past Blame, the great feeling-killer.

Forgiveness is not a reflex reaction. After I've been wronged, it takes time to go through the process of experiencing the hurt; being angry about it; mourning it; then moving to understanding, forgiveness and healing.[10]

my morning walk and meditation with the Lord's Prayer. Two lines in particular change the way I view the world:

> Forgive me my wrongs,
> As I forgive those who wrong me.[11]

These words inexplicably change my day. They change the way that I deal with people that cut me off in traffic — as well as people that bruise my heart. They remind me that I make mistakes, and so do those around me. Yet, all of us travelers on Spaceship Earth deserve forgiveness. We all merit grace.

"Forgive me my wrongs, as I forgive those who wrong me" reminds me that hurt is inevitable in life, and that:

- I am imperfect and wrong others.
- Others are imperfect and wrong me.
- I will be forgiven, for the asking.
- In turn, I can forgive those who wrong me.
- I obtain forgiveness for myself at the same time as I forgive others.

"Forgive me...as I forgive..." — the two processes are inextricably linked.[12]

This transforms my world.

For example, if someone cuts me off in traffic, I'm tempted to call him a jerk. If I'm carrying around unresolved feelings, I may unload on him — and guide him to the proper lane with my middle finger. If I repeat a grievance story about him, I can upset myself for hours.

But if I take the time to recall *my wrongs* (and the many times I have accidentally cut people off), my perspective shifts. I am not his victim and he is not my tormentor — we're all just bozos on this bus. This is his turn to goof up, but mine is coming soon.

I've discovered that if I give him a break and smile at him as he cuts ahead of me, I'm also giving myself a break. For I not only avoid upsetting myself in that smiling moment. I also make my next driving mistake far easier. When *I* cut somebody off later on, I imagine that person will be as forgiving as I've been. Curiously, he usually is. If not, I give *myself* the gift of peace by forgiving that too. As a result, I now drive a far easier road.

The fact is that the more forgiving I am of others, the more forgiving I am of myself. St. Francis had it right: "It is in pardoning that we are pardoned."[13]

There is a physiological explanation for this. The lower brain — source of our vivid emotions — lacks a direct connection to the outside world. When it responds to symbols generated by the cerebral cortex, it assumes that all behavior is inner-directed. Therefore, when I am generous and forgiving with another person, my lower brain assumes this cerebral activity is intended for me and responds with positive emotion.[14]

Thus, when I give grace to others, I actually give it to myself — physiologically, as well as theologically.

Similarly, when I am blaming toward another person, my lower brain assumes the blame is for me and responds with negative emotions. Thus, giving blame to others is giving it to myself. This is why people often experience a negative "hangover" after getting angry and blaming. As St. Francis might have put it: "It is in blaming that we are blamed."[15]

In the end, perhaps this is the most compelling argument for forgiveness. Blame, like grace, is indivisible. What we do unto others, we actually do to ourselves.

The Country of Love

Love is an act of endless forgiveness,
a tender look which becomes a habit.
— Peter Ustinov

And so I begin to learn forgiveness. Now when I make a mistake, I try to forgive myself:

I pause and picture a Kind Father putting his arm around my shoulder, offering forgiving words: "I know you've made a mistake and that's not desirable. Let's try to change that in the future. But for now it's OK, bud." I go forward unburdened.

On a good day, I can treat others just as tenderly. As the Kind Father accepts my flaws, I can accept the flaws in others. It works something like this:

(Kind Father) accepts ⟶ **(Me) I accept** ⟶ **(Myself) I accept** ⟶ **(Others)**

The Technology of Forgiveness

The Lord's Prayer works for me. But the Stanford University Forgiveness Project has developed a scientific program that teaches people how to forgive. Dr. Luskin argues that forgiveness is a choice and it can be learned.

First, he says, you must meet the preconditions for forgiveness:
- Get clear on what happened and what's wrong.
- Get clear on your feelings.
- Share your feelings.

This is consistent with my experience. It's vital for me to get in touch with my emotions first — because alienation from my own feelings is what drives my addiction to blame.

After meeting the above preconditions, Luskin teaches people to:
- Recall what I hoped for and what my positive intention was. (e.g., "Before the divorce, I wanted a happy marriage and intended to be a good husband and father.")
- Remind myself that I can't always get what I want — that hurt and disappointment is part of everyone's life. Luskin teaches people to challenge the self-talk that says things should be different. "Shoulds" are at the heart of every toxic grievance story.
- Instead of saying, "She should have done this" change it to: "I had hoped she would do this." This keeps me in touch with my own feelings of disappointment, instead of vainly trying to assert control over another person. It keeps my focus on me and my feelings, instead of blaming her.
- Stop endlessly repeating the Grievance Story. I may be constantly tuned in to the "Grievance channel" on my mind's TV screen — giving the "bad guy" massive amounts of air time. But I can take him off the air. There are other available channels. For example, I

When I do this, I catch a glimpse of the land that Robert Karen describes as the "Country of Love." In this country human beings are seen as a mixture of good and bad, but still worthwhile. All sorts of regrettable things can happen in this country, without making me worthless — or turning you into my tormentor. Damage happens, but I am confident it can be repaired. I experience hurt, process it and move on. Eventually, in this country, I will forgive.[16]

In the Country of Love, forgiveness is not just a single act

---

can change to the "Natural Beauty channel," by focusing on the beauty of a tree, a bird, a sunset. If I concentrate on appreciating beauty rather than grievance, I soon feel more positive and forgiving.

Alternatively, I can tune into the "Gratitude channel." If I focus on counting all the good things in my life, I leave less mental space for grievances. The same is true if I focus on the channel of "What kindness can I do for someone today?"[17]

The point is, I can choose to stop focusing compulsively on grievance.

• Perhaps most important, affirm that I can still apply my original positive intention. ("Although she left me, I will still be a good father. And this is the way I will do it, as a separated father.")

Affirming my continuing positive intention is key. This allows me to again tell the narrative of my life as hero, no longer as victim. Victims can only blame — heroes can move on with positive goals, positive lives.

The Stanford method works. The Forgiveness Project actually taught people from Northern Ireland how to forgive terrorists who had killed their family members. The people practicing these techniques became psychologically healthier, reduced their stress levels, felt less hurt and angry, more optimistic, more compassionate and self-confident. They reported an improved quality of life, with more control over their emotions.[18]

Indeed, forgiveness begins to work quickly. Studies show that people who go through an exercise of simply visualizing that they are forgiving their nemesis show immediate improvement in their cardiovascular function.[19]

of mercy for an individual wrong. It's "a tender look which becomes a habit." It's a worldview. It's a way of life.

The forgiving worldview is based on this premise: I will respectfully assert my boundaries, and I will ask others to change actions that offend me. But when things are still not as I hoped, I will choose to move forward positively. I will accept and process the feelings I have, and not escape from them by endlessly blaming them on you. I will make peace with the past and move on.

I will choose to see life's problems as opportunities for growth and learning. Instead of railing on about what *should* have been, I will live in the world that is. I will set aside pre-conceptions about what my life *should* be — so that I can enjoy the life that actually lies before me.

Every day I will count my blessings, rather than my grievances.

Forgiving Dad

For a long time, I hated my dad and didn't forgive him. I hated him for his drinking, his rages, his vulgarity — for walking around the house in his underwear, for peeing in the bathroom sink, for scaring me. When I was 13, I wished he would die. And then he did.

I thought I had killed him. For fifteen years I never mentioned his name to anyone. Applying kid's magical thinking, I was scared to death I might kill someone else with mere thoughts. For the longest time I couldn't forgive myself. I was scared to death that I would damage someone else.

But I'm healing. And as I write this chapter and explore the idea of forgiveness, I think of Dad... his father dying at about the time that boys are first forbidden to feel their emotions, at age five... publicly humiliated by his preacher grandfather in front of the congregation at 14... then running away from home and living on his own... adventuring to Alaska, becoming a bush pilot... later a glad-handing California salesman, a

Willie Loman, a man's man... a man finally undone by unemployment, drinking and failure.

Dad never took the first step towards forgiveness — he never got in touch with his own pain, never knew how to process his own tender feelings. Instead he took the Anger Path, and forced those unwanted feelings onto us. He blamed himself for feeling forbidden pain, then quickly shifted that blame onto us. He took us all to live in the Country of Resentment.

Eventually he drank and blamed the forbidden feelings away. And he killed himself in the process. But he wasn't always like that. A memory returns:

It was evening at the river. I was five, and Dad was still young and strong. We were camping in the California Coast Range. Although I couldn't swim, I had wandered down to the river after dinner, and paddled an inner tube out to the middle of the big dark pool. I lay back in the inner tube, gazing at the cliff that loomed above, on the other side of the water.

Suddenly I slipped through the middle of the tube, and I was in the water, struggling. I sank into the cold dark water. As I struggled to the surface, I could see my dad running down the beach, tearing off his shoes, and plunging powerfully into the river. Then I was under again, swallowing cold water, sinking into blackness....

In a moment I was pushed powerfully to the surface. He had come up below me, pushing me to the air. As I gasped for air, he rose like a sea lion to the surface below me and I was saved.

But then he swallowed water and began to cough and struggle himself. "Dad!" I cried in a panic. He sank below me and I again fell back into the black waters, gulping and sputtering, stepping on his head. As we sank, the murky yellow light of the world receded into darkness, with no sound but my thundering heartbeat.

I felt his hands grip my calves and place my feet firmly on his shoulders. Then, as in the game we'd often played, he drifted down and bounced back up from the river bottom, thrusting me to the surface. And then his tattooed arm was around my chest, towing me

to safety. Keeping my face above the water, he coughed, then murmured, "It's OK, Cal. It's OK."

Finally we staggered onto the little sandy beach, and Dad hugged
me. As I stood gasping, shivering and crying, he hugged me to his
heaving chest. Then he went over and got a towel out of the trailer
and wrapped it around me.

Later, as he heated hot chocolate on the Coleman stove he did
the unusual — he sat me on his lap. After a while, he turned the Gi-
ants game on the radio, and we sipped hot chocolate while the sun
sank behind the cliff.

By the end, I think Dad, like me, had totally forgotten that
day. He forgot his goodness. I wish that, when he ruminated
on his failures, he had been able to remember the good things.
I wish that, when he thought of his years of unemployment,
his bankruptcy, the jalopies he drove, his failed marriages, his
destructive anger, he had been able to recall that day on the
river. Most of all, I wish he'd had a Kind Father to remind
him of the good things about himself — his sense of humor,
his charm, his ability to spin a story for a crowd, his compassion for the unfortunate, his intelligence, his ability to make a
day's outing with a young boy into an exciting adventure.

I wish he had understood that he was no different than
any of us, a mixture of good and bad. I wish someone had
told him that he didn't have to be a superhero, he was simply
human. I wish he had realized that he could be forgiven, and
that he could forgive.

The fact was, he didn't have to die alone in the Country
of Resentment. There was room for him in the Country of
Love.

Journey
to a
Man's Heart

Dad, 1957.

Epilogue

The Hero Revisited

Again his mother leads the young Theseus through the forest to introduce him to his father. Once again they discover the granite stone by the emerald lake. But this time when the young man shoves the massive stone aside, he not only finds armor and sword — he finds something he missed before. Hidden in the chest plate in a small leather pouch is a cloth bag filled with coins and a short, carefully-drawn note. The note says:

To my son,
Remember this
No matter what happens, I will always love you.
Dad

Theseus reads the note slowly, and stares out over the lake. Then he reads the note again. Passing one of the coins to his mother, he stands up and carefully folds the note into the pouch, then puts the pouch back into the armor.

He hugs his mother good-bye, puts on the armor and sets out to find his father. Again he crosses a dark and dangerous land. But this time he is not alone.

This time when he confronts the villains in the wilderness, he senses his father at his side. As he wrestles Sciron on the cliff top, he hears his father's voice: "You can do it, son. You'll be OK. You can take him." With relief, he hurls the monster into the abyss. When the Pine Bender lashes him to the killing trees, Theseus summons his father's strength and breaks free. When he falls asleep in the lonely waste-land only to be wakened by howling wolves, he lies in the dark and clutches the pouch.

This time when Theseus arrives in Athens, his father joins the crowd that welcomes the new hero. This time, Theseus immediately tells the King who he is. Instead of offering his son a cup of poisoned wine, the King offers him the best wine in the kingdom.

Father and son stay up feasting and drinking all night long. Theseus tells his father about growing up at his mother's palace — about the goats he raised, about his friends, about exploring the nearby forest. And about what it was like to not have a father. Dawn finds them without armor, standing on the balcony watching the sun rise. Theseus turns to his father and tells him about the note — and how he carries it with him everywhere. Moved, the King finally tells his son how he missed him, how much he cared for him. He apolo-gizes, and hugs Theseus.

It's still not easy. Theseus must still save Athens. He still has to enter the labyrinth alone, face its dark horrors and kill the Minotaur. But this time when he returns to Athens, he is not drunk — he re-members his father and replaces the ship's black sails with his father's white ones. As a result, the father understands the son's message. Instead of throwing himself off the cliff in despair, the King climbs down to welcome his son and dress his wounds.

Many years later, when the King lies dying, Theseus comes to his bedside. The young man sits quietly with his father, and holds his hand. At the end, he bends over the failing man and whispers gently in his ear. The old man smiles, then nods off, breathing raggedly.

When the room darkens, the young man lights a candle, and takes out the worn leather pouch. He removes the ancient note, care-fully unfolds it and studies it for a long time. As tears track down his face, he sits still by his father's tremulous body.

Then, furrowing his brow, Theseus finally writes a few halting words on the paper. He puts it back into the pouch. Then he tender-ly slides the pouch under his father's shirt, until it rests over the old man's heart.

When his father finally dies, Theseus rushes to the mountain top, where he sobs and rails at the sky. But this time he doesn't fall into the abyss. This time he returns to the palace to hold his own infant son.

His father is with him always.

Glimpses of a Kind Father

In the end, Dad returns from the shadows, borne on a flood of memory. Today I remember a Kind Father — the father before the drinking and the rage, before I was old enough to be trained to "be a man."

I am five years old, and we're driving the big, black 1950 Packard through the cool Central Valley night. Dad and I hurtle through blackness, our cocoon lit only by faint dashboard light and cigarette glow. The radio crackles. Hank Williams fades in and out on the "K-R-A-K Krack Corral of Country Hits."

The heater's on high, wind whistles in through the lowered window. Propping my pillow against the passenger door, I gaze out at the sky. I lie back, pull the army blanket over me, and fall into the bowl of darkness and stars.

After a while, the cigarette lighter clicks metallically, and pops out of the dash. I sit back up. Dad reaches over and brings the glowing red spiral up to his face. The cigarette flames up, illuminating the crags of his face, the face I wear decades later, as I write this.

Flooded rice paddies stretch out endlessly into the dark. The red lights of radio towers glow in the distance, foothills the shape of a woman's body rising behind them. In the cozy Packard, Hank Williams sputters to life:

Well, why don't you love me like you used to do
How come you treat me like a worn out shoe
My hair's still curly and my eyes are still blue
Why don't you love me like you used to do?

Dad reaches into his shirt pocket and wordlessly hands over a Tootsie Roll. I take the surprise and quickly unwrap it.

"What do you think Tom and the babies are doing right now, champ?"

I try to respond, but my mouth is full of the chewy candy. "Probably asleep, I'd guess," he answers for me. "It's up to us men to go and find us a new house, huh?" He pauses. "You're going to like living in Paradise." He reaches over and tousles my hair. I nod and smile.

Well, why don't you be just like you used to be
How come you find so many faults with me
Somebody's changed so let me give you a clue
Why don't you love me like you used to do?

Dad hums along. He finishes his cigarette, and flips it out the window, sparks streaming into the night.

Abruptly, the pitch of the engine changes as we enter a tunnel of trees. The yellow headlights illuminate rows of almond trees. A gust of wind blows blossoms and the hint of almond extract smell across our path. Just as suddenly we're back out to prairie again. Static overwhelms the radio. Dad fiddles with the dial for a minute, bringing the song back:

Why don't you say the things you used to say
What makes you treat me like a piece of clay
My hair's still curly and my eyes are still blue
Why don't you love me like you used to do?

The static rises again. "Dammit," Dad says softly. After trying the dial again, he turns it off.

"Hey, son, do you know any songs?"

"I know Three Blind Mice. Mrs. Smith taught it to us."

So I sing the song for him:

Three blind mice, three blind mice
See how they run, see how they run
They all run after the farmer's wife....

"SHE CUTS OFF THEIR TAILS WITH A BUTCHER'S KNIFE!" Dad interjects,
and we finish together:

Did you ever see such a sight in your life
As three blind mice?

On the last word, Dad snorts with satisfaction. It's quiet for a few minutes, just the sound of the engine, the heater, tires slapping the road. After a while, Dad looks over at me and smiles. Holding his gaze for a moment, I lay my cheek against the back of the cloth-covered bench seat. A pair of oncoming headlights pulls his gaze away. He squints, looking down the highway. "You want to hear a new song?"

"OK."

"Now this is a very, very serious song."

"OK."

"My Uncle Simon taught this song to me when he came back from Africa." Dad looks over at me seriously. I've never heard of Uncle Simon. Grinning, Dad sweeps his hand briefly over his glossy, combed back hair, and starts to sing, in a powerful, smooth tenor:

Boom-boom, ain't it great to be crazy
Boom-boom, ain't it great to be crazy
Silly and foolish all day long
Boom-boom, ain't it great to be crazy!

On "boom-boom", he slaps the chrome dash playfully. At the end, he vibrates his lips to make an engine noise.

"Now you try it."

"OK." We sing the chorus together. On "boom-boom", he reaches over and softly taps my head.

We decelerate as we pull into a small farming community. A single street light casts pale light on cinderblock buildings, a few houses recede into the dark. The car engine strains as we stop for the stop sign. The town is empty, as if we are the only ones on earth.

As he accelerates, back onto the open road, Dad looks over at me again. "OK, now try this:

A horse and a flea and three blind mice
Sitting on a tombstone, shooting dice

The horse fell off and landed on the flea
Whoops said the flea, there's a horse on me!

I laugh, and try to repeat the verse, but I miss a few words. He fills them in, then we sing it together. On the chorus, his voice becomes so loud it's a bit scary.

Way down deep in darkest Africa
A mouse stepped on an elephant's toe
The elephant looked down with tears in his eyes...

Dad stops for a beat, then delivers the punchline falsetto,
WHY DON'T YOU PICK ON A FELLA YOUR SIZE!

I giggle, and he laughs, slapping my knee softly. He sings the song over again, until I know all the words. Then we sing it several more times. Each time now, he sings "boom-boom" like a drum.

I yawn. "You cold?" Dad asks. He puts out his arm, and I shift over to snuggle up next to him as he drives.

I lay against his side, against the bulk and the warmth of him, feeling the tide of his breath; smelling his aftershave and smoke as the Packard hurtles down the highway. As I fall asleep, he's humming softly.

When we get to the hotel, I wake up when Dad turns off the car. "You awake?" he asks. I say nothing, pretending to sleep. He picks me up and carries me to our room, holding me close as he walks up the stairs. My cheek against his soft cotton shirt, I smell his sweat, feel the beating of his heart. He puts me down on the bed, and kisses me on the cheek. His whiskers are rough on my skin. "Good night, slugger," he whispers.

Recommended Readings

Highly Recommended

The Courage to Raise Good Men, Olga Silverstein and Beth Rushbaum. Viking, 1994.

The Dance of Anger, Harriet Lerner. Perennial Currents, 2005.

Feeling Good: The New Mood Therapy, David Burns. Avon, 1980.

Forgive for Good, Fred Luskin. Harper, 2003.

The Forgiving Self: The Road from Resentment to Connection, Robert Karen. Anchor, 2003.

Getting the Love You Want, Harville Hendrix. Owl, 2001.

How to Be an Adult in Relationships: The Five Keys to Mindful Loving, David Richo. Shambala, 2002.

How to Be Your Own Best Friend, Mildred Newman, Bernard Berkowitz and Jean Owen. Ballantine, 1971.

I Don't Want to Talk About It, Terrence Real. Fireside, 1998.

Nonviolent Communication: A Language of Life, 2nd ed., Marshall Rosenberg. PuddleDancer, 2003.

Real Boys, William Pollack. Owl, 1999.

The Road Less Travelled, M. Scott Peck. Touchstone Simon & Schuster, 2003.

Understanding and Managing Your Anger and Aggression, Bud Nye. BCA, 1993.

Recommended

Anger is Not an Emotion, Jeanette Kaspar. BeYou, 2001.

Anger Kills, Redford and Virginia Williams. Times, 1993.

The Anger Management Sourcebook, Glenn Schiraldi and Melissa Kerr. Contemporary McGraw Hill, 2002.

Beyond Anger: A Guide for Men, Thomas Harbin. Marlowe & Co., 2000.

Forgive and Forget, Lewis Smedes. Harper Collins, 1996.

Forgiveness: How to Make Peace With Your Past and Get on With Your Life, Sidney and Suzanne Simon. Warner, 1991.

How Can I Get Through to You? Closing the Intimacy Gap between Men and Women, Terrence Real. Scribner, 2002.

The Male Stress Syndrome, Georgia Witkin-Lanoil. Berkley, 1988.

No Future Without Forgiveness, Desmond Tutu. Doubleday, 1999.

Prisoners of Hate, Aaron Beck. Perennial Harper Collins, 2000.

The Six Pillars of Self-Esteem, Nathaniel Branden. Bantam, 1995.

Something More: Excavating Your Authentic Self, Sarah Ban Breathnach. Warner, 2000.

NOTES

Chapter 1: Patriarchy's Price

1. Jack Meyer. "Improving Men's Health." *American Journal of Public Health* 93 (May 2003), pp. 709–712.
2. William Pollack. *Real Boys.* Owl, 1999, p. 341.
3. "Men's Health and Worksite Health Promotion." [online]. [cited July 26, 2006]. imt.net/~randolfi/healthy men/ and National Council for Alcoholism and Drug Dependence. "Use of Alcohol and Other Drugs Among Women." [online]. [cited July 26, 2006]. ncadd.org/facts/ women.html; also *American Journal of Public Health* 93 (May 2003), p. 724 and following.
4. Sanjay Gupta. "Why Men Die Young." *Time Magazine* Vol. 161 #19 (May 12, 2003).
5. Georgia Witkin-Lanoil. *The Male Stress Syndrome.* Berkley, 1988, p. 39. Nearly three out of four heart attacks before age 65 strike men (Will Courtenay. "Constructions of Masculinity and Their Influence on Men's Well-Being." *Social Science and Medicine* 50 (2000), p. 1385). Also see the articles found in the *American Journal of Public Health* 93 (May 2003).
6. *The Male Stress Syndrome*, p.51.
7. David Williams. "The Health of Men: Structured Inequalities and Opportunities." *American Journal of Public Health* 93 (May 2003), p. 724 and following.

8. Usually at the hands of other men (Olga Silverstein and Beth Rushbaum. *The Courage to Raise Good Men.* Viking, 1994, p. 240).

9. According to Daniel Kruger, a social psychologist at the University of Michigan Institute for Social Research. (Daniel Kruger and Randolph Nesse. "Sexual Selection and the Male:Female Mortality Ratio." [online]. [cited July 13, 2006]. *Evolutionary Psychology.* 2:66–85 (June 2004). human-nature.com/ep/articles/epo26685.html).

10. Herb Goldberg. *The Hazards of Being Male.* Signet, 1987, pp. 108–109; Elizabeth Barrett-Connor, M.D. "Sex Differences in Coronary Heart Disease: Why Are Women So Superior?" *American Heart Association Journal.* 1997; 95:252–264; and "Macho Attitude Shortens Men's Lives." *USA Today Magazine.* September 1997, Vol. 126, Issue 2628. For the connection between male anger and heart attacks, see the discussion in chapter six.

11. David Williams. "The Health of Men: Structured Inequalities and Opportunities." *American Journal of Public Health* 93 (May 2003), p. 724 and following. See the other articles in the same journal on the topic of men's health.

12. For example: W.H. Courtenay. "Constructions of Masculinity and Their Influence on Men's Well-Being: A Theory of Gender and Health." *Social Science and Medicine.* 50 (2000), pp. 1385–1401; W.H. Courtenay. "College Men's Health: An Overview and Call to Action." *Journal of American College Health.* May 1998, Vol. 46, Issue 6, p. 279; and M.C. Davis. "Is Life More Difficult on Mars or Venus." *Ann Behav Med.* 21 (1999), pp. 83–97.

In addition to the matters discussed here, the masculine role encourages men to engage in risky behavior, engage in fewer health-promoting behaviors, sleep less, take fewer precautions (*e.g.*, seat belts, sunscreen) and refuse to seek out medical and emotional help when needed.

13. Including manic and depressive episodes, generalized anxiety, panic disorder, social and other phobias, substance abuse, and antisocial personalities (Terrence Real. *I Don't Want to Talk About It.* Fireside, 1998, pp. 41 and 84). Note that covert depression can be exhibited in a variety of ways, including drinking, workaholism, angry outbursts, controlling behavior, etc.

14. *I Don't Want to Talk About It*, p. 146.

15. Dr. Henrie Treadwell, Kellogg Foundation Program Director for Health, made these remarks at the launch of the Foundation's national campaign to deal with the "Silent Crisis in Men's Health". See the July 21, 2003 Kellogg Foundation News Release and associated materials at wkkf.org.

16. Steve Biddulph. *Manhood,* 2nd ed. Finch Publishing, 1995, p. 6. In Canada and Australia, the divorce rate is about 40%, but the rate is higher in the US.

17. See Real's book, *I Don't Want to Talk About It.*

18. Michael Gurian discusses how male and female brains developed differently because of the different tasks that men and women faced in the ancient world (Michael Gurian. *Boys and Girls Learn Differently.* Jossey-Bass, 2001, pp. 38–41). Gurian argues that because ancient males had to routinely kill for hunting and war that this led to the male brain de-emphasizing emotive, verbal and empathy skills.

19. English has many words to condemn men who show the "feminine" characteristic of sensitivity ("wimps," "sissies," "wusses," "pussies") but almost none to condemn sensitive women. Conversely, we have numerous words to condemn women who show strength and anger ("shrews," "bitches," "nags," "witches," "castrators") but almost none to condemn strong, angry men (Harriet Lerner. *The Dance of Anger.* Perennial Currents, 2005, p. 2).

20. Thanks to Terrence Real for this apt phraseology.

21. Sam Keen. *Fire in the Belly.* Bantam, 1992, p. 208.

22. See the works of Carl Jung and Terrence Real on this subject. Psychologist Emmy Werner's research shows that the more that people incorporate both traditionally male and female attributes, the more likely they are to deal successfully with life situations. (James Garbarino. *Lost Boys*. Anchor, 2000, p. 169.)

23. *Real Boys*, p. 6.

24. Pollack cites the work of Professors Deborah David and Robert Brannon in this regard (*Real Boys*, pp. 23–25).

25. *Globe and Mail*, January 17, 2005, p. A14.

26. See the works of Carole Gilligan, William Pollack, Terrence Real and Olga Silverstein for descriptions of how boys are pressured to reject their emotional selves.

27. Bridget Murray, quoting Dr. Niobe Way. "Boys to Men: Emotional Miseducation." [online] [cited July 14, 2006]. *APA Monitor*. Vol 30 #7 (July/August 1999). apa.org/monitor/julaug99/youth.html; also Robert Pasick. *Awakening from the Deep Sleep*. Harper San Francisco, 1992, p. 12.

28. As Olga Silverstein puts it, "Sooner or later, usually by the end of the teen years, this incessant denial [of boys' feelings] will spell the death of feeling." (*The Courage to Raise Good Men*, p. 118).

29. *Real Boys*, p. xxii.

30. *I Don't Want to Talk About It*, p. 181.

31. Thanks to John Bradshaw for the apt term, "human doing."

32. Rabbit's girlfriend Ruth says this in Updike's book, *Rabbit at Rest*. Random House, 1992.

33. Samuel Osherson. *Finding Our Fathers*. Contemporary Books/McGrawHill, 2001, p. 4.

34. *Finding Our Fathers*, p. 4.

35. *Manhood*, p. 39.

36. See *The Courage to Raise Good Men* for a discussion of this dynamic.

Chapter 2: Saying Goodbye to the Harsh Father

1. *Newsweek*, January 16, 2006, p. 65.
2. Michael Adams. *Fire and Ice: The United States and Canada and the Myth of Converging Values.* Penguin Canada, 2003, p. 50; *Vancouver Sun*, July 30, 2005, p. C-1. It's interesting to note that the percentage of Canadians that support that statement is far lower (18%) than the percentage of Americans that support it (49%). This reflects a profound difference in gender attitudes between the two countries.
3. See Chapter One for the studies that document the large number of men who had angry and distant fathers, and the relatively small number who had encouraging fathers.
4. Bertrand Russell, as quoted in Thomas Harris. *I'm OK — You're OK.* Avon, 1973.
5. See Mildred Newman, Bernard Berkowitz and Jean Owen. *How to Be Your Own Best Friend.* Ballantine, 1971, p. 38.
6. *I Don't Want to Talk About It,* p. 198.
7. As Carl Jung pointed out. See the discussion of this Jungean principle in Guy Corneau. *Absent Fathers, Lost Sons.* Shambhala, 1991, p. 36.
8. *I Don't Want to Talk About It,* p. 227.

Chapter 3: Discovering the Kind Father

1. *How to Be Your Own Best Friend*, pp. 66, 88 and 90–91.
2. Ibid., p. 86.
3. Robert Karen. *The Forgiving Self: The Road from Resentment to Connection.* Anchor, 2003, pp. 74–75.
4. As the pre-eminent psychologist Carl Jung noted, "Nothing has a stronger influence psychologically on their environment and especially on their children than the unlived life of the parent." See quotationsbook.com/com/authors/3902/Carl_Jung.

5. Psychologists such as Abraham Maslow and Albert Ellis have described how self acceptance is a prerequisite for self-actualization.
6. Excerpted from Dorothy Law Nolte and Rachel Harris. *Children Learn What They Live.* Workman, copyright 1998, Introduction. The poem "Children Learn What They Live" copyright 1972 by Dorothy Law Nolte. Used by permission of Workman Publishing Co., Inc., New York. All rights reserved.

Chapter 4: Looking Inside

1. Adapted from *The Wizard of Ox*, by Frank Baum. Note that the Wizard's final comment cited here is found in the movie version, not the book.
2. T. S. Eliot. "The Hollow Men" from the *Selected Poems of T. S. Eliot.* Harcourt, Brace and Company, 1958.
3. Compulsive/addictive behaviors keep me out of relationship with my self. The wide spectrum of addictive behaviors, from workaholism to heroin addiction, are all ways to avoid feelings and evade self. Anne Schaef provides a penetrating discussion of how people use addictive behaviors to avoid self (Anne Schaef. *When Society Becomes an Addict.* HarperCollins, 1988).
4. See Chapter Five for a discussion of how a good listener helps one discover one's feelings. As Paul Tournier puts it in *The Meaning of Persons* (Buccaneer, 1999), "We become fully conscious only of what we are able to express to someone else. We may already have a certain intuition about it, but it must remain vague so long as it is unformulated."
5. See Thomas Harbin. *Beyond Anger: A Guide for Men.* Marlowe & Co., 2000, pp. 48–49. Harbin points out that women have a much broader vocabulary for emotional states, presumably because they have more practice at identifying and describing emotions. Just as Inuit

have many words for "snow" because they pay close attention to that phenomenon, women have many words for emotions because they pay closer attention to their inner landscape. The estimate that close to 80% of men have difficulty identifying what they are feeling is that of psychologist Ronald Levant, cited in *I Don't Want to Talk About It*, p. 146.

6. When I talk to myself about the background situation that led to the feeling, I try the same approach. I try to avoid using aggressive metaphors and language in describing the situation. I know that if I say, "We had a big fight," that gets me more agitated than saying, "We had a disagreement." If I say the businessman is holding "a gun to my head," that causes me to react more intensely than if I say, "He's negotiating aggressively." I try to avoid the cognitive distortions that David Burns describes in his classic book, *Feeling Good* (Avon, 1980). For example, I try to avoid catastrophizing, making negative generalizations about myself, labelling myself and others, and jumping to unsubstantiated conclusions about what others are thinking about me.

7. Medical science has confirmed the healthful effects of such emotional release. As Nathaniel Branden puts it in *The Six Pillars of Self-Esteem* (Bantam, 1995), p. 92: "Experiencing our feelings has direct healing power."

8. Abraham Maslow noted that self-actualizing individuals have "superior awareness of their own impulses, desires, opinions and subjective reactions in general" (Abraham Maslow. *Motivation and Personality*. HarperCollins, 1987). Psychotherapist Arno Gruen has made a similar point: "Autonomy entails having a self with access to its own feelings and needs"(*The Courage to Raise Good Men*, p. 126). Furthermore, in his classic work on *Emotional Intelligence* (Bantam, 1995), Daniel Goleman argued that awareness of one's own feelings is an absolute

prerequisite for emotional intelligence. Such awareness allows you to express your feelings appropriately, and to be empathetic. And emotional awareness is also a prerequisite for healthy self-esteem. Nathaniel Branden notes that self-esteem *begins* with listening to your body and emotions — having a relationship with self (*The Six Pillars of Self-Esteem*, Chapter Six, "The Practice of Living Consciously").

9. *How to Be Your Own Best Friend*, p. 72.

10. St. Augustine. "Wonder..." [online]. [Cited July 24, 2006]. allspirit.co.uk/augustine.html.

Chapter 5: Speaking What I Feel

1. See Chretien de Troyes, *Percival or The Holy Grail* and the interpretation of the ancient legend put forward in *Absent Fathers, Lost Sons*, pp. 137–9. For a discussion of the different versions of this legend, see *The Quest, an Arthurian Resource* (uidaho.edu/student_orgs/arthurian _legend/welcome.html).

2. See the discussion and statistics about these male maladies in Chapter One. We commit suicide at four times the rate of women, and our heart attack rate is approximately double, until we hit old age. Scientists have linked men's refusal to turn to friends during crises to our higher heart attack rates and shorter lives.

3. Romans 12:15; Ephesians 4:15.

4. This paraphrases Sarah Breathnach's recounting of the traditional story. See Sarah Ban Breathnach. *Something More: Excavating Your Authentic Self.* Warner Books, 2000, pp. 259–260.

5. Kahlil Gibran. *A Tear and a Smile.* Quoted in Arthur Ciaramicoli and K. Ketcham. *The Power of Empathy.* Dutton Adult, 2000, Introduction.

6. M. Scott Peck. *Further Along the Road Less Travelled.* Touchstone, 1998, p. 28. I am indebted to Marshall Rosen-

berg for ideas in this section on how people don't listen. I highly recommend his books on empathetic listening, including *Nonviolent Communication: A Language of Life,* 2nd ed. (PuddleDancer, 2003).

7. See Marshall Rosenberg's discussion of this seminal statement of Buber's at the website of PuddleDancer Press, nonviolentcommunication.com/rosenberg/nvc-topics .htm.

8. David Richo. *How to Be an Adult in Relationships: The Five Keys to Mindful Loving.* Shambala, 2002.

9. Theologian Paul Tillich (1886–1965), quoted in *O Magazine,* February 2004.

10. Various studies confirm that in sharing the stressful event, I am likely lowering my cardiac risk. See Redford and Virginia Williams. *Anger Kills.* Times , 1993, pp. 58–60.

11. *Vancouver Sun,* November 2, 2005, p. A-12, citing the *National Geographic,* November 2005.

12. Pearl S. Buck quoted in M. Scott Peck. *Abounding Grace: An Anthology of Wisdom.* Ariel Book, 1996, p. 279.

Chapter 6: Anger: Escape from Feeling

1. Adapted from Herman Melville, *Moby Dick*.

2. See Dr. Glenn Schiraldi and Dr. Melissa Kerr, *The Anger Management Sourcebook,* Contemporary McGraw Hill, 2002, p. 2 and following for a discussion of this broadly accepted concept.

3. Psychiatrist Jean Baker Miller describes the phenomenon: "It is particularly common to find men acting most aggressively when they feel vulnerable, hurt, frightened and alone" (*The Courage to Raise Good Men,* p. 132). For a description of the physiology of the anger response, see Dr. Redford Williams and Dr.Virginia Williams, *Anger Kills,* Times Books, 1993, pp. 26–29. Once angry, we lose the ability to clearly think and perceive our feelings (John Gottman. *Why Marriages Succeed or Fail.* Simon

and Schuster, 1994, p. 116). The fight-or-flight response
originates in the lower brain, and during this response the
primitive amygdale — the "emergency-response" brain
— takes over from the cortex (Jeanette Kasper. *Anger is
Not an Emotion.* BeYou, 2001, pp. 13–26).

It is interesting to note that while society teaches men
to convert vulnerable feelings into anger, it has traditionally taught women to do the opposite. Women have been
encouraged to ignore even justifiable anger and replace it
with sadness. Perhaps this is why books on anger for men
talk about controlling anger — and books for women talk
about the need to identify and express it. Under patriarchy we are, indeed, "two halves of a crippled whole."

4. See the movie *Dirty Harry*, starring Clint Eastwood.

5. Re: heart attack and stroke risks: High anger men over-
   secrete stress hormones which damage heart muscles and
   cells lining blood vessels, make blood platelets stickier,
   weaken the immune system and raise cholesterol. The
   overall death rate of such men is significantly higher. A
   study of Finnish men showed that those who regularly
   expressed high levels of anger had more than twice the
   risk of stroke than men that were more laid-back (*Anger
   Kills,* pp. 25–40; *The Readers' Digest*, April 2004, p. 58;
   and *Beyond Anger*). On the other hand, those who can
   move away from chronic anger can literally save their
   own lives. A Stanford University study showed that heart
   attack patients who learned to reduce their controlling,
   aggressive and hostile behaviors reduced the rate of recurrent heart attacks by half. Those who use cognitive
   methods to reduce their anger lower their blood pressure
   as much as those who take blood pressure medication
   (Aaron Beck. *Prisoners of Hate.* Perennial Harper Collins, 2000, p. 283; and the *Anger Management Sourcebook*, p. 26).

   Re: Accident Risks: See the study by Daniel Vinson of

the University of Missouri-Columbia, reported in *The Globe and Mail*, February 8, 2006, p. A18.

6. As the American Psychological Association has stated: "Expressing your angry feelings in an assertive — not aggressive — manner is the healthiest way to express anger. To do this, you have to learn how to make clear what your needs are, and how to get them met, without hurting others. Being assertive doesn't mean being pushy or demanding, it means being respectful of yourself and others" (American Psychological Association. "APA Topic: Anger." [online]. [cited August 2, 2006]. apa.org/topics/ topicanger.html).

   Timely assertiveness actually avoids the root of much anger. If you set reasonable limits early on, you avoid the situation of failing to set limits until the person steps on your toes one time too many — a sure recipe for a blow-up.

7. Because angry blame triggers the other person's defensiveness, it seldom leads to a good resolution. Instead, as described by Harriet Lerner, angry blame triggers a dance that actually reinforces a dysfunctional status quo (*The Dance of Anger*, pp. 55–57).

8. See Bud Nye. *Understanding and Managing Your Anger and Aggression*. BCA, 1993, pp. 3-15 to 3-23 for a discussion of how you can invoke anger to distract yourself from painful emotions, but how it ends up preventing you from taking care of yourself.

9. Epictetus, *The Enchiridion*.

10. *Prisoners of Hate*, p. x.

11. Angry actions (e.g., yelling, gesticulating) can intensify thoughts and bodily responses even more. This dynamic between thoughts and body response has been called the "anger feedback loop." See Henrie Weisinger. *Dr. Weisinger's Anger Work-Out Book*. Quill, 1985, pp. 29–32. Also, see *Why Marriages Succeed or Fail*, p. 116.

12. In *The Anger Management Sourcebook*, Dr. Glenn Schiraldi describes how repeatedly getting angry sensitizes the nervous system, so that subsequently it takes less irritation to trigger a stress/anger response (pp. 55–56). Apparently the brain itself can change to reflect habitual emotional responses. See Daniel Goleman, *Destructive Emotions,* Bantam, 2004, p. 288 where Paul Ekman, University of California at San Francisco Medical School Professor of Psychology, mentions how the brain learns negative behavior. In conversation with the Dalai Lama, Professor Ekman describes how acting cruelly actually changes the brain over time.

13. See *Prisoners of Hate,* pp. ix–xii, 25–50 and 71–90.

14. See the *Anger Management Sourcebook,* pp. 55–56 (discussed in footnote 12). Also, see p. 18 for mention of the fact that anger deadens vulnerable feelings.

15. M. Scott Peck. *The Road Less Travelled.* Touchstone, Simon and Schuster, 2003, p. 50.

16. Cognitive behavior theory explains why focusing on one's own feelings keeps one from becoming angry. See Aaron Beck's explanation in *Prisoners of Hate,* p. 258.

17. Jack Kornfield. *A Path With Heart.* In Gillian Stokes. *Forgiveness: Wisdom from Around the World.* MQ Publications, 2002, p. 95.

18. Kahlil Gibran. *The Prophet.* Knopf, 1985, p. 29.

19. See the discussion earlier in this chapter of Aaron Beck's theory regarding this.

20. Thich Nhat Hanh. *Anger.* Riverhead, 2002, p. 125.

21. Once the heart rate gets to 100 beats per minute, adrenaline floods in and creates the "fight or flight" response. Then you can't accurately hear what the other person is saying because this response engages the more primitive amygdala part of the brain that responds to emergencies, instead of the cortex. Psychologist John Gottman recommends that people should agree to take a "time out" from

an argument when one's heart beats per minute (BPM) reach 10% above normal (an increase of 8–10 BPM). The "time out" should be at least 20 minutes, to let hormones flush out of the body (*Why Marriages Succeed or Fail*, pp. 116 and 176–8; and *Anger is Not an Emotion*). Interestingly, Gottman notes that men become overwhelmed by feelings more quickly than women (*Why Marriages Succeed or Fail*, pp. 145–149).

22. Plutarch urged this anger management approach over two thousand years ago: "For he who gives no fuel to fire puts it out, and likewise he who does not in the beginning nurse his wrath and does not puff himself up with anger, takes precautions against it and destroys it" (*Understanding and Managing Your Anger and Aggression*, p. ix).

23. Anthony Robbins. *Awaken the Giant Within*. Free Press, 2003, p. 212.

24. Kenneth Byers. *Who Was That Masked Man Anyway?* Journeys Together, 1993, p. 33.

Chapter 7: Forgiveness and Freedom

1. See *The Forgiving Self*, where Robert Karen contrasts two fundamental world views — those who live out their lives in a Country of Resentment, and those who see themselves living in a Country of Love.

2. Fred Luskin. *Forgive for Good*. Harper, 2003, pp. 15 and 79. See Chapter Four of Luskin's book for a description of how grievance stories work.

3. *Forgive for Good*, pp. xv and 78–81. In Chapter Seven Luskin presents a general discussion of the health impacts of nonforgiveness.

4. Desmond Tutu. *No Future Without Forgiveness*. Doubleday, 1999, p. 272.

5. *The Forgiving Self*, p. 112. "The More We Blame, The Farther We Get From Ourselves" is Karen's title for Chapter Six of the same book.

6. Lewis Andrews. *To Thine Own Self Be True*. Main Street Books, 1989, p. 9.

7. *Romeo & Juliet* V. III. 291–293

8. *New Oxford English Dictionary*, 1998, s.v. "forgiveness".

9. See Sidney and Suzanne Simon. *Forgiveness: How to Make Peace With Your Past and Get on With Your Life*. Warner, 1991; and *Forgive for Good*.

10. See Lewis Smedes. *Forgive and Forget*. Harper Collins, 1996; *Forgiveness: How to Make Peace With Your Past and Get on With Your Life*; and *Forgive for Good*.

11. Note that Today's English Version of the *Bible* uses the word "wrongs" where other translations use the word "trespasses" or "sins".

12. In *Forgive and Forget*, Lewis Smedes describes this inextricable link between feeling forgiven and being able to forgive another (see p. 120).

13. *The Prayer of Peace*, St. Francis of Assisi, 1182–1226.

14. Harville Hendrix. *Getting the Love You Want*. Owl, 2001, pp. 9, 10, and 170–171.

15. This psychological truth was also reflected in Matthew 7:1 "Judge not, lest ye be judged".

16. See *The Forgiving Self*, Chapter Four (particularly at p. 77) for this description of the Country of Love.

17. See *Forgive for Good*, Chapter Nine, for a description of how to "change channels" to focus on beauty, gratitude, love and kindness instead of grievance. Focusing on gratitude has long been viewed as a key to a happy life. Centuries ago Dr. Samuel Johnson pointed out: "The habit of looking on the best side of every event is worth more than a thousand pounds a year" (quoted in Dale Carnegie, *How to Stop Worrying and Start Living*. Simon and Schuster, 1984, p. 142). Similarly, focusing on being kind beats focusing on grievance. Doing something kind for another person is a classic mood elevator. In fact, it was

listed as one of top eight tips for making yourself happy in *Time*, January 17, 2005, pp. A8–A9.

18. *Forgive for Good*, pp. xvi–xvii and Chapters Seven and Eight.

19. *Forgive for Good*, p. xv. Forgiving a grudge also appears to lower blood pressure in hypertension patients (*Forgive for Good*, p. 81).

About the Author

HOLLY PATTISON

CALVIN SANDBORN was born in Alaska to a bush pilot father and social worker mother. He grew up in Northern California, where his mother became the state's "Social Worker of the Year" — and his father became a traveling salesman and drank himself to death.

Mr. Sandborn has spent his adult life in Canada, first as a community organizer and adult literacy teacher. Over the last twenty-five years he has become one of British Columbia's leading environmental lawyers. Currently he is a law professor at the University of Victoria, where he teaches public interest advocacy and supervises the noted Environmental Law Clinic.

He is a well-known freelance journalist, publishing on a wide variety of topics. This memoir and guide is enriched by the author's years of research into psychology, gender issues and self-help, and by his participation in a weekly men's group.

Calvin Sandborn lives in Victoria, British Columbia with his daughters and grandson.

If you have enjoyed *Becoming the Kind Father*
you might also enjoy other

BOOKS TO BUILD A NEW SOCIETY

Our books provide positive solutions for people
who want to make a difference. We specialize in:

Environment and Justice • Conscientious Commerce
Sustainable Living • Natural Building & Appropriate Technology
Ecological Design and Planning • Educational and Parenting Resources
Nonviolence • Progressive Leadership • Resistance and Community

For a full list of NSP's titles, please call **1-800-567-6772**
or check out our website at:

www.newsociety.com

NEW SOCIETY PUBLISHERS

Our books provide positive solutions for people who want to make a difference.

For a copy of our catalog, please mail this card to us.

We specialize in the following; please indicate your area/s of interest:

- ❏ Activism
- ❏ Globalization
- ❏ Ecological Design & Planning
- ❏ Environment & Economy

- ❏ Conscientious Commerce
- ❏ Sustainable Living
- ❏ Environmental Education
- ❏ Education & Parenting
- ❏ Progressive Leadership

- ❏ Conflict Education
- ❏ Storytelling
- ❏ Natural Building & Renewable Energy
- ❏ Making a Difference

❏ *Please subscribe me to* NEW SOCIETY NEWS — *our monthly e-mail newsletter.*

Name_____

Address/City/Province_____

Postal Code/Zip_____Email Address_____

toll-free 800-567-6772   **www.newsociety.com**

NEW SOCIETY PUBLISHERS

Our books provide positive solutions for people who want to make a difference.

For a copy of our catalog, please mail this card to us.

We specialize in the following; please indicate your area/s of interest:

- ❏ Activism
- ❏ Globalization
- ❏ Ecological Design & Planning
- ❏ Environment & Economy

- ❏ Conscientious Commerce
- ❏ Sustainable Living
- ❏ Environmental Education
- ❏ Education & Parenting
- ❏ Progressive Leadership

- ❏ Conflict Education
- ❏ Storytelling
- ❏ Natural Building & Renewable Energy
- ❏ Making a Difference

❏ *Please subscribe me to* NEW SOCIETY NEWS — *our monthly e-mail newsletter.*

Name_____

Address/City/Province_____

Postal Code/Zip_____Email Address_____

toll-free 800-567-6772   **www.newsociety.com**

NEW SOCIETY PUBLISHERS

NEW SOCIETY PUBLISHERS
P.O. Box 189
Gabriola Island,
B.C. V0R 1X0
Canada

NEW SOCIETY PUBLISHERS
P.O. Box 189
Gabriola Island,
B.C. V0R 1X0
Canada